W9-ANO-960

Les Petits Sweets

LES PETITS SWEETS

TWO-BITE DESSERTS FROM THE FRENCH PÂTISSERIE

Kathryn Gordon and Anne E. McBride

RUNNING PRESS
PHILADELPHIA • LONDON

Copyright © 2016 by Kathryn Gordon
and Anne E. McBride
Photographs copyright © 2016 by Evan Sung
Published by Running Press
An Imprint of Perseus Books,
A Division of PBG Publishing, LLC,
A Subsidiary of Hachette Book Group, Inc.

All rights reserved under the Pan-American
and International Copyright Conventions

Printed in China

This book may not be reproduced in whole or in part, in any form or by any means, electronic or mechanical, including photocopying, recording, or by any information storage and retrieval system now known or hereafter invented, without written permission from the publisher.

Books published by Running Press are available at special discounts for bulk purchases in the United States by corporations, institutions, and other organizations. For more information, please contact the Special Markets Department at the Perseus Books Group, 2300 Chestnut Street, Suite 200, Philadelphia, PA 19103, or call (800) 810-4145, ext. 5000, or e-mail special.markets@perseusbooks.com.

ISBN 978-0-7624-5728-1
Library of Congress Control Number: 2016934182

E-book ISBN 978-0-7624-5729-8

9 8 7 6 5 4 3 2 1
Digit on the right indicates the number of this printing

Designed by Frances J. Soo Ping Chow
Edited by Kristen Green Wiewora
Food styling by Jessie Riley and Kathryn Gordon
Typography: Baskerville No2, Brandon, Isabelle Script, Maxwell Slab, and Morva

Running Press Book Publishers
2300 Chestnut Street
Philadelphia, PA 19103-4371

Visit us on the web! www.offthemenublog.com

Contents

Introduction

WHETHER FOR A TOURIST OR A LOCAL, RARELY A DAY GOES BY IN FRANCE without a visit to a favorite bakery or pastry shop. There's a baguette to pick up, perhaps a cake for a dinner party, some petits fours to bring to a friend's home, an afternoon treat for the kids' *goûter*. Colorful stores greet visitors with a pyramid of nougats or a glass case filled with jewel-like pastries, for an explosive sensory experience. While always in moderation, sweets are central to the French way of life.

They are central to my life as well. At the Institute of Culinary Education, I teach professional and recreational pastry classes and get to have a lot of fun with both while always researching the latest techniques and flavor combinations and coming up with new courses. I talk about emulsions and baking theory with my colleagues. I create new fillings based on what is available during a class. I experiment with everything from miniature treats, perfect on mignardise trays in fancy restaurants, to the full-size versions of classic desserts that my students come back to try time after time.

Anne and I both go to France every year—to different regions, which allows us to see trends from a broader perspective. We visit as many shops as we can while there and try as many desserts as possible, taking bites and notes in equal proportions. We take inspiration from the work of the country's best pastry chefs and accidental discoveries in a neighborhood's bakery.

One thing we have noticed from eating our way around France is the overwhelming presence of two-bite treats, at home and in restaurants or pastry shops. My own experience with bite-size pastries goes back to my early days in the kitchen, when it was often the job of the newbie to make nougats or financiers that guests would enjoy at the end of the meal. It was a fun chance to practice my skills and at times even invent flavor combinations, to stretch my creativity a bit while on the lowest rung on the ladder.

Two bites: It's about moderation but also about sophistication and elegance—two very French traits. We wanted to explore the mini-sweets, from the ones that are traditionally petite to smaller servings of true classics. Our first book, *Les Petits Macarons*, offered dozens of unique macaron recipes, and came out just as the United States was waking up to these best-known French treats. This book includes some of my new macaron creations, but is far more expansive, with recipes for financiers, tartelettes, petits fours, savarins, and much more that will transform any home kitchen into the most sophisticated of pâtisseries. You'll find such confections as pâtes de fruits—fruit-based grown-up gumdrops—plus marshmallows, caramels, and cookies and pastries with crunchy and soft textures. While the inspiration is French, the flavors come from all over the world, in pairings that range from classic to contemporary.

My hope is that *Les Petits Sweets* will become the one source you turn to when looking to add to your dessert table, your party, or your hostess gift. Don't get me wrong—I love cakes, pies, and full-size tarts and tortes just as much. But what I appreciate when making two-bite desserts is that my guests can try more of them. There's no need to choose, and that allows me to cater to more tastes at once. For a small dinner party, I can serve something in the favorite flavor of everyone at the table. A guest loves chocolate; another, pecan; a third, passion fruit? No problem, I can create three easy treats that will make them each feel like the most important person at my table. When I'm hosting something larger, or baking in a restaurant setting, small-scale desserts give me one last chance to leave a guest with just the perfect flavor combination, capping off a beautiful experience. It's about making everyone feel special. The ultimate refinement, of course, is to put a few of those small treats in a box or confectionery bag and hand those out to guests as they leave; treats that can be made ahead are perfect for that purpose, since they give off perfect host(ess) vibes without additional stress.

This is a book to get you in the kitchen, making treats that are as delectable as they are beautiful. Two bites can pack a lot of flavor punch, leaving behind the sweetest taste memory. One that will linger long after the last crumb is dusted, leaving you with the satisfaction of being the most satisfying baker in town.

Licorice sticks

Baking Tips

THE RECIPES IN THIS BOOK CONTAIN A SLEW OF TECHNIQUES, TIPS, AND NOTES TO ensure that you bake with great success. Anne and I want you to make each treat, love it, and adopt it as a favorite, serving it over and over again. To offer just a bit of extra help, this chapter includes some more baking tricks that come up frequently over years of baking and teaching classes, whether it is to professional students or amateur bakers. Read them before you start baking and refer to them when suggested throughout the book.

BAKE BY WEIGHT: Professional bakers use scales for consistent measurement, because what one person might measure when scooping a cup of flour or sugar will be different from the next—you might go deeper in the bag and shake it more, for example, aerating the flour and thus filling the cup with less of it. Different brands of measuring cups and spoons can also lead to different measurements. Basic digital kitchen scales are now widely available for around $30. Buy one with 5-gram accuracy.

Some measurements in this book are for fewer than 5 grams—spices, for example. You can purchase a small precision digital scale (available online for about $10), which will measure only up to about 100 grams in total, but has the great advantage of measuring down to 0.5 gram. You can bake without such a scale, however, using incremental measuring. Instead of zeroing out the weight of the container after measuring each ingredient, for example 100 grams of sugar and 1 gram of ground cinnamon, measure the sugar and then add the cinnamon until the scale goes up to 101 grams.

CHECK YOUR OVEN'S TEMPERATURE: Buy an inexpensive oven thermometer and check your oven for any hot spots. That will tell you where a dish might brown faster and how you should turn it in such cases. If your oven temperature runs high, you might need to adjust the temperature of a recipe by reducing it by 25°F (4°C) or decrease the total baking time.

ADJUST FOR CONVECTION: If you are baking with a convection oven (the at-home kind, not the commercial bakery kind), deduct 25°F (4°C) from the recipe's stated baking temperature.

CALIBRATE YOUR CANDY THERMOMETER: You'll notice that the instructions call for a calibrated candy thermometer. A difference of just a couple of degrees will change the state of a sugar syrup and thus the final recipe, which might end up too firm or too soft, so make sure that the thermometer you are using is as accurate as possible. To calibrate it, insert your candy thermometer in boiling water. If it's not there yet, use a towel to move the glass adjuster until it is at the 212°F (100°C) mark. When cooking a syrup, the temperature of the sugar often jumps around. To ensure an accurate reading, wait until the thermometer holds the desired temperature for 1 minute.

PICK THE RIGHT SAUCEPAN SIZE: In this book, a small saucepan holds 1.5 quarts and measures 6 inches (15 centimeters) in diameter. A medium saucepan holds 4 quarts and measures 8 inches (20 centimeters) in diameter. It is important to use a saucepan that is deep enough and of the correct width for the recipe, especially when cooking honey syrups and candies. Otherwise, the syrup may overflow or the sugars may crystallize, changing the desired result of the candy.

IF YOU WHISK OR BEAT IN A SMALL QUANTITY OF EGG WHITES OR EGGS: When whisking just one or two egg whites or beating one egg or yolk in a regular-size electric mixer, the whisk or paddle attachment might not touch the egg. You can loosen the attachment so that it drops as it turns and reaches the egg, or you can lift the bowl (which requires you to hold it) to obtain the same result. When loosening the whisk, raise it back up and attach it correctly once the egg whites start to turn to foam, to prevent damage to the wires.

WHIP EGG YOLKS TO THE RIBBON STAGE: When making a batter, egg yolks and sugar are often whipped to the ribbon stage. Place the yolks and sugar in the bowl of an electric mixer set with the whisk attachment and turn the mixer to high speed. When the mixture turns a pale, light yellow color and has tripled in volume, reduce the mixer speed to medium-low speed for 2 minutes. This will stabilize the size of the air bubbles and prevent the batter from deflating in the oven. To check that it is ribboning correctly, stop the mixer and let some of the mixture drip off the whisk. If it clearly "ribbons" on top of itself (as if you were dropping fabric ribbon) or holds a three-dimensional shape for 3 seconds, it is ready. If not, keep whipping on low speed until it does.

CREAM YOUR BUTTER AND SUGAR: Creaming works the best with room-temperature ingredients, especially the butter and eggs. What needs to happen is called an emulsion, which is mixing together the fat and water molecules in ingredients. With room-temperature ingredients, and mixing time (a paddle attachment for a mixer is perfect), the fat in the butter (or cream cheese) will emulsify with the water molecules in the butter. You will then more easily be able to slowly incorporate eggs and any other liquids (such as milk) into the butter.

ALTERNATE DRY AND WET INGREDIENTS: When baking cakes, alternating dry and wet ingredients is a typical procedure that prevents the overdevelopment of gluten. Add the dry ingredients one quarter at a time (eyeballing the quantity is fine) into the mixer and mix until barely combined. Add the wet ingredients one third at a time, letting them trickle down the side of the bowl with the mixer on low speed, mixing until barely combined each time. Add each batch as soon as the other one is incorporated, to limit the time the mixer is running, or you'll risk

Cannelé Molds

overmixing the batter. If needed, stop the mixer and scrape the sides of the bowl with a spatula to ensure that everything is mixing homogenously.

IF YOUR BATTER SEPARATES: When mixing a batter, it might at times look as if it were separating and more wet than normal. Keep mixing it a bit longer to homogenize before adding any other ingredient; this will prevent overmixing once the flour is added, which would overdevelop the flour's gluten—not a desirable result for cakes and cookies. Mix until the mixture is "fluffy," which means until it forms a homogenous, soft mass, with nothing clinging to the sides of the bowl or the paddle (typically 5 to 10 minutes). Feel the bottom of the bowl; it should not be cold. If necessary, let the ingredients already in the batter mix and come to room temperature a bit longer before adding anything else, and the batter will recover from this separation.

PIPE BATTERS AND FILLINGS: From making the perfect macaron shell to filling a small mold with precision, piping comes in handy in a variety of applications. Some require the use of specific tip shapes and sizes (easily available at kitchenware and craft stores, as well as online), but in most instances you can also cut the tip of a disposable piping bag in the specified size, being careful to use a sharp knife or scissors, and cut straight across. A clean cut ensures that the filling or batter then flows out of the bag cleanly and precisely. If no dimension is specified, a ¼-inch (6-millimeter) tip or cut will work with anything but the chunkiest of batters or fillings. If using a tip, make sure to cut the pastry bag so the pattern in the tip is just exposed, or you won't obtain the desired shape while you pipe. Spoon what you want to pipe into a pastry bag, filling it only two thirds of the way so that you can then have a good grip on the bag when piping. Tie the bag closed to keep the batter from oozing out of the top.

BAKE COOKIES IN BATCHES: A few cookies in this book are slice and bake, but the majority are piped. In some cases, not all cookies in one recipe will fit on one baking sheet. If that's the case, keep the batter wrapped and chilled until the first batch has baked. If your oven can fit two baking sheets at once and bake evenly, prepare everything at once and load it up. If not, bake in two batches.

CHOP YOUR CHOCOLATE: I use chocolate pistoles, which are larger than chocolate chips and exist in the same varying degrees of chocolate as their whole counterparts. Most pistoles are sold by distributors to professionals, so in large quantities only, but you will be able to find them online. Don't substitute chocolate chips, which may contain artificial fats to hold the chip shape; therefore, they resist melting evenly. Rather, use the best chocolate you can find or afford, buy it as a block or bar, and chop it up in a food processor or with a chef's knife on a cutting board. The weight of the chocolate won't vary much between whole and chopped. When finely chopped is indicated, make sure to do so, since it's what will allow the chocolate to melt.

MAKE GANACHE: Finely chop the chocolate. When making small batches, as here, I use a food processor to ensure that the chocolate pieces are small enough to fully melt in a small amount of liquid. For the best texture, boil the cream in a pot big enough to hold both the cream and the chocolate. When the cream comes to a boil, remove it from the heat and shake in the chocolate to submerge it. The residual heat from the pan will melt the chocolate, and this method prevents a lumpy ganache. Let the chocolate sit in the pot for 1 minute before stirring, so that the cocoa butter (a.k.a. fat) in the chocolate becomes hot enough to fully melt. Whisk quickly from the center of the pot only, to create an emulsion. When the chocolate mixture is shiny in the center of the pot, whisk the remainder, starting from the center to the outside of the pot—imagine a spiral staircase.

MELT CHOCOLATE OVER A DOUBLE BOILER: Bring a pan filled halfway with water to a boil over medium-high heat. Lower the heat to low, and place the measured and chopped chocolate in a stainless-steel bowl that can fit over the pan without touching the water. Let the chocolate melt halfway before you stir it with a heat-resistant spatula. Be careful not to let steam escape from under the bowl (lower the heat if this threatens to happen) or to let water splatter into the bowl, or the chocolate will seize. It will take about 5 minutes, but pay close attention, particularly if melting a small amount of chocolate, so that it doesn't burn. You can also use a double boiler to bring components of a dish back to the right consistency, as you will see noted in a number of recipes.

AVOID SUGAR CRYSTALLIZATION: When making a caramel or a candy that starts by melting sugar into a syrup, ensure that your saucepan, tools, and granulated sugar are clean and free of debris. Place the sugar in the middle of the pan. Pour the water around the edges of the pan, toward the center in a spiral motion to dissolve the sugar. Only stir if the recipe instructs you to do so and avoid the edges of the pan by slowly stirring in the shape of a figure-eight with a heat-resistant spatula, staying about ½ inch (1.25 centimeters) away from the sides of the pan. As a sugar syrup boils, all the ingredients mix together naturally; you should not interfere with the process by stirring unless instructed to do so. If needed use a clean pastry brush and cool water to clean the sides of the pot by dipping the brush in the water and working around the pot circumference. Do not dip the brush in the syrup. Clip a calibrated candy thermometer to the side of the pan and cook to the indicated temperature.

COOK FRUITS IN SYRUP: When cooking fruits in syrup, you may need to add a bit of water to cover them, depending on the size of your pan. The syrup should always cover the fruit by ¼ to ½ inch (6 millimeters to 1.25 centimeters). If you see it evaporating or if a great deal of white foam forms, remove the pot from the heat and add more water.

After you have finished cooking the fruits and have used them in a recipe, pour a little bit of the leftover syrup over ice cubes in a glass and top with seltzer for a slightly sweet, refreshing drink.

WORK WITH GELATIN SHEETS: Gelatin sheets need only to be rehydrated in ice water to be incorporated in a recipe. Sheets are more precise, too. "Silver" and "gold" refer to different strength levels; they are available online (see Resources, page 288). Submerge the sheets in ice water for 3 minutes; the gelatin should feel limp when it's time to remove it. Remove any excess water with a sieve, then proceed with the recipe. If you have warm hands, or if the kitchen is warm, you can inadvertently melt some of the gelatin and it won't set the recipe correctly, so be careful. For most of the recipes here, I call for gold gelatin sheets. Some recipes, such as those for marshmallows (pages 251–262), use granulated gelatin—the main reason, as unscientific as it sounds, is that this is how I've always done it and it works. Granulated gelatin and gold gelatin sheets generally have the same gelling strength by weight.

ZEST CITRUSES THE RIGHT WAY: To zest an orange, grapefruit, lemon, lime, or other citrus fruit without collecting any of the bitter white pith, use a Microplane zester. Hold the citrus in your nondominant hand and the zester in your dominant hand. Carefully draw the Microplane from the top of the citrus to the bottom, turning the fruit as you go.

TOAST NUTS AND SEEDS: Preheat the oven to 350°F (175°C). Spread the nuts or seeds on a baking sheet and bake them until they are toasted through, about 6 minutes. To check that they are done, break one open and taste it. The oil content varies depending on the type of nut or seed, so if you start to smell them earlier, trust your nose and open one up to check—they might be ready. Because their oil content varies, it is best to use separate pans for toasting multiple types of nuts, so that none of them burn.

USE LEFTOVER VANILLA BEANS: In many recipes throughout this book, you are instructed to rub the seeds of a vanilla bean into sugar to extract its flavor. Once you've done that, the "used" vanilla bean can be turned into vanilla sugar. Dry the beans for at least 1 day by leaving them out and uncovered, then place ½ cup (115 grams) of granulated sugar per each half vanilla bean in the bowl of a food processor with the vanilla bean(s) and pulse on and off for 5 minutes, until you obtain a well-combined powdery sugar. Sift the sugar through a fine-mesh sieve to remove any remaining vanilla bean bits. Use this sugar to add sweetness and flavor to tea, oatmeal, and any dish you'd like, or in place of vanilla extract and some of the sugar when baking.

USE GOLD LEAF: To give a tartelette or petit four a sophisticated finished appearance, decorate it with a touch of edible gold leaf. Gold is edible at 23 carats, although 24 carat is commonly available. You will find it online or in specialty cake decorating stores (see Resources, page 288).

Orange-Hazelnut Financiers

FINANCIERS

ORANGE-HAZELNUT FINANCIERS

TANGERINE-POPPY FINANCIERS

COFFEE-CARDAMOM FINANCIERS

CASHEW-CURRY FINANCIERS

I FIRST ENCOUNTERED FINANCIERS DURING MY FIRST JOB IN NEW YORK, AT THE Rainbow Room. The long lineage of French pastry chefs there made it a haven for this rich and easy treat. It takes only minutes to prepare but can take on a variety of flavors and shapes. These nut-based bite-size cakes are made with beurre noisette, a delicious browned butter. The flavor of the financiers is greatly improved by letting the batter rest in the refrigerator overnight. At times I even "age" it for up to three days. Financiers belong to the pound cake family and can be traced back to the nineteenth century. Legend has it that they owe their name to their shape—that of a gold bar. Silicone financier molds, which reflect that rectangular shape, are now widely available, but you can bake them in any mold you'd like as long as its cavities are small. A mini-muffin pan also works. Fill the mold cavity three quarters of the way up since the financiers will expand a bit while baking. Cake flour gives the financiers a lighter texture, allowing them to almost dissolve on the tongue; all-purpose flour would make them toothier.

BEURRE NOISETTE

Noisette is the French word for "hazelnut." Here, it refers to the nutty flavor and brown color that the butter acquires during the cooking process. The amount below is what you need for the recipes in this chapter, but it's easy enough to make 1 or 2 pounds (455 or 905 grams) of beurre noisette at a time. If you make a large batch, spread the melted butter in a shallow pan to cool, then cut it into four equal portions. Store each portion in a resealable plastic bag for ease of use, keep it frozen or refrigerated, and remelt it before using.

4 tablespoons (56 grams) unsalted butter, cut into cubes

Heat the butter in a medium saucepan over medium-low heat until it melts and turns a deep, nutty color. Do not stir the mixture or swirl the pan. Carefully strain the beurre noisette into a container through a fine-mesh chinois sieve to separate the fat from the settled milk solids. If you are not sure that your sieve is fine enough, line it with a coffee filter, cheesecloth, or paper towel to trap the browned milk solids as you strain.

Orange-Hazelnut Financiers

Almond and hazelnut flours are staples of the French pastry kitchen. Here, you can find it in the baking or health food aisle, or online (see Resources, page 288). Hazelnut flour's distinctive flavor makes here for a complex financier, paired with orange confit and Grand Marnier—a treat unquestionably for the grown-ups at the table.

Makes about 24
(2-inch/5-centimeter) financiers

2 cups (216 grams) hazelnut flour

⅓ cup plus 1 tablespoon (45 grams) cake flour

½ cup (90 grams) confectioners' sugar

½ teaspoon (2 grams) fine sea salt

6 large egg whites

1 tablespoon (15 grams) Grand Marnier

Finely grated zest of 1 orange (about 8 grams)

¼ cup (45 grams) orange confit,
finely diced (see page 270)

3 tablespoons (42 grams) Beurre Noisette
(see facing page), melted and kept warm

Vegetable oil cooking spray

Place the hazelnut flour, cake flour, confectioners' sugar, and salt in the bowl of a food processor and pulse for 10 seconds, or until the mixture is fine and powdery. Transfer it to a mixing bowl. Stir in the egg whites, Grand Marnier, zest, and orange confit until everything is completely mixed, then stir in the beurre noisette until just incorporated. Cover the batter and refrigerate it overnight.

Preheat the oven to 400°F (200°C). Spray a metal or silicone financier mold with vegetable oil cooking spray.

Spoon the batter into a piping bag and cut a ¼-inch (6-millimeter) opening in the bag, straight across. Pipe it into the mold's cavities until they are three-quarters full. Bake for 10 minutes, until the financiers puff up in the center and are light brown on the edges. Unmold immediately onto a wire rack and repeat until the batter is used up. They will taste best if eaten the same day.

Variation

TANGERINE-POPPY FINANCIERS

Substitute the finely grated zest of 3 tangerines (12 grams) for the orange zest and omit the orange confit. Add 1 tablespoon (15 grams) of poppy seeds with the flour. Substitute 1 tablespoon (15 grams) of Amaretto for the Grand Marnier.

Coffee-Cardamom Financiers

Coffee and cardamom have deep flavors that are very complementary—I like adding a tiny bit of cardamom to ground coffee when I'm brewing a pot and looking for something that will jolt my taste buds. And not that it needs to be specified, but serve these financiers with coffee, of course!

Makes about 24
(2-inch/5-centimeter) financiers

2 cups (216 grams) almond flour

½ cup plus 1 teaspoon (95 grams) confectioners' sugar, divided

⅓ cup plus 1 tablespoon (45 grams) cake flour

1 tablespoon (3.5 grams) espresso powder

1½ teaspoons (2 grams) ground cardamom

½ teaspoon (2 grams) fine sea salt

6 large egg whites

1 teaspoon (4 grams) pure vanilla extract

3 tablespoons (42 grams) Beurre Noisette (see page 24), melted and kept warm

Vegetable oil cooking spray

Place the almond flour, ½ cup (90 grams) sugar, cake flour, espresso powder, cardamom, and salt in the bowl of a food processor and pulse for 10 seconds, or until the mixture is fine and powdery. Transfer it to a mixing bowl. Stir in the egg whites and vanilla until everything is completely mixed, then stir in the beurre noisette until just incorporated. Cover the batter and refrigerate it overnight.

Preheat the oven to 400°F (200°C). Spray a metal or silicone financier mold with vegetable oil cooking spray.

Spoon the batter into a piping bag and cut a ¼-inch (6-millimeter) opening in the bag, straight across. Pipe it into the mold's cavities until they are three-quarters full. Bake for 10 minutes, until the financiers puff up in the center and are light brown on the edges. Unmold immediately onto a wire rack and repeat until the batter is used up. Just before serving, place the remaining teaspoon (5 grams) confectioners' sugar in a small mesh sieve and gently tap the sugar over the financiers. They will taste best if eaten the same day.

Cashew-Curry Financiers

I love making my own curry powder and think that it makes a difference in a recipe, since I can tailor it exactly to my favorite spices and always ensure that the spices are at their freshest when I grind them. So, a recipe follows for you to make your own, should you desire, but store-bought curry powder will work as well. I like the warmth that this curry-cashew combination offers. It's an usual financier that will keep your guests talking long after the last bite.

Makes about 24
(2-inch/5-centimeter) financiers

1⅓ cups (206 grams) cashews, toasted (see page 20) and coarsely chopped

½ cup (90 grams) confectioners' sugar

⅓ cup plus 1 tablespoon (45 grams) cake flour

1 teaspoon (2.8 grams) curry powder

½ teaspoon (2 grams) fine sea salt

6 large egg whites

1 teaspoon (4 grams) pure vanilla extract

3 tablespoons (42 grams) Beurre Noisette (see page 24), melted and kept warm

Vegetable oil cooking spray

Place the cashews in the bowl of a food processor and pulse in 5-second increments about 10 times, scraping the bowl a few times. Add the sugar, flour, curry powder, and salt and pulse 10 more times, or until the mixture is fine and powdery. Transfer it to a mixing bowl. Stir in the egg whites and vanilla until everything is completely mixed, then stir in the beurre noisette until just incorporated. Cover the batter and refrigerate it overnight.

Preheat the oven to 400°F (200°C). Spray a metal or silicone financier mold with vegetable oil cooking spray.

Spoon the batter into a piping bag and cut a ¼-inch (6-millimeter) opening in the bag, straight across. Pipe it into the mold's cavities until they are three-quarters full. Bake for 10 minutes, until the financiers puff up in the center and are light brown on the edges. Unmold immediately onto a wire rack and repeat until the batter is used up. They will taste best if eaten the same day.

CURRY POWDER

This recipe makes more than you need for the financiers, but will store for three months. You can increase the quantities, too, to make a big batch at once and offer a small jar of it alongside the financiers for a unique hostess gift.

Makes about 3 tablespoons (25 grams)

1 teaspoon (1.5 grams) coriander seeds

1 teaspoon (3.8 grams) ground turmeric

1½ teaspoons (4.3 grams) cumin seeds

1 teaspoon (6.5 grams) whole fenugreek

½ teaspoon (1.4 grams) red pepper flakes

½ teaspoon (1.5 grams) ground ginger

½ teaspoon (1.5 grams) garlic powder

½ teaspoon (2.2 grams) yellow mustard seeds

¼ teaspoon (0.5 gram) ground cardamom

⅛ teaspoon (0.3 gram) ground mace

⅛ teaspoon (0.5 gram) freshly grated nutmeg

¼ teaspoon (1 gram) ground cinnamon

Pulse all the spices together in a spice grinder or clean coffee mill until fine, then sift them. Store in an airtight jar in a dark cabinet for up to 3 months.

Black Pepper–Sour Cream Madeleines

MadeleineS

BLACK PEPPER–SOUR CREAM MADELEINES

LEMON-ANISE MADELEINES

CHESTNUT MADELEINES

PEAR-ROSEMARY MADELEINES

BANANA–BROWN SUGAR MADELEINES

FIG-FENNEL-MASCARPONE MADELEINES

THANKS IN PART TO MARCEL PROUST, MADELEINES ARE, NEXT TO MACARONS, probably the most well-known French treat. Their soft texture and the slight bit of magic it takes to get that perfect signature peak are other reasons for their popularity. Madeleines are best fresh out of the oven, but no one will mind the last-minute work when rewarded with warmth and delicateness. Prepare the batter one day in advance and chill it in the fridge. The contrast between the chilled batter and the burst of heat when you place the mold in the oven helps create the aforementioned peak. You can purchase both silicone and metal madeleine molds; I haven't found a real difference in results between the two types, so use what you prefer. I used "regular"-size molds here, which typically make twelve madeleines, but you can also make mini madeleines with smaller molds. For those, decrease the baking time by one minute and pay close attention to your oven in case you need to pull them out early, since they'll bake faster. To check that they are cooked, break one of the thicker madeleines in half—the baker's treat, all in the name of proper verification.

Black Pepper–Sour Cream Madeleines

You may have read that sprinkling black pepper on strawberries heightens their flavor—it's true! You might not taste the pepper, but will certainly feel its presence. The same happens with these madeleines. You will not eat them thinking that black pepper and sour cream belong on a baked potato; rather, you will marvel at the imperceptible elements that make them unique. And in the summer, do indeed serve them alongside cut-up ripe strawberries, for a simple but memorable dessert.

Makes 12 large madeleines

6 tablespoons (84 grams) unsalted butter

⅓ cup (67 grams) granulated sugar

1 vanilla bean

2 large eggs

¾ cup (190 grams) sour cream

½ cup (68 grams) all-purpose flour

⅓ cup (40 grams) almond flour

¾ teaspoon (3 grams) baking powder

½ teaspoon (2 grams) freshly ground black pepper

¼ teaspoon (1 gram) fine sea salt

Vegetable oil cooking spray

Place the butter in a small saucepan over medium heat and let it melt. Remove from the heat and let it cool slightly.

Place the sugar in the bowl of an electric mixer. Split the vanilla bean lengthwise and scrape out the seeds with the back of a paring knife into the sugar. Fit the mixer with the whisk attachment, set the bowl, add the eggs to the sugar, and whisk until the mixture reaches a ribbon stage, where the whisk leaves a strong, three-dimensional shape.

Whisk a little bit of the egg mixture into the sour cream to loosen it, then add the sour cream to the mixing bowl and whisk until combined.

Remove the bowl from the mixer and fold in the all-purpose flour, almond flour, baking powder, pepper, and salt until just combined, about 30 seconds. Fold in the melted butter. Spoon the batter into a piping bag (do not cut an opening yet), tie the bag closed, and refrigerate the batter overnight.

Preheat the oven to 425°F (220°C). Spray a nonstick 12-cup madeleine pan with vegetable oil cooking spray.

Cut a ¼-inch (6-millimeter) opening straight across the tip of the pastry bag. Pipe the madeleine batter into each cavity of the pan, filling it nearly to the top. Immediately place the pan in the hot oven and bake for 10 to 11 minutes, or until the edges of the madeleines are golden and their top is puffed up. Remove from the oven and unmold immediately by inverting the pan onto a wire rack. Eat the same day.

Lemon-Anise Madeleines

The scents of lemon and anise by nature always make me want to stop what I'm doing for a second, sit down for tea, and think about new recipes. These soft and highly aromatic madeleines push that feeling even further, and are the perfect complement to a cup of strong black tea.

Makes 12 large madeleines

6 tablespoons (84 grams) unsalted butter

3 large eggs

⅓ cup (67 grams) granulated sugar

4 packed teaspoons (16 grams) finely grated lemon zest (from 4 lemons)

½ cup (68 grams) all-purpose flour

⅓ cup (40 grams) almond flour

1½ teaspoons (4 grams) aniseeds

¾ teaspoon (3 grams) baking powder

¼ teaspoon (1 gram) fine sea salt

Vegetable oil cooking spray

Place the butter in a small saucepan over medium heat and let it melt. Remove from the heat and let it cool slightly.

In the bowl of an electric mixer fitted with the whisk attachment, whisk the eggs, sugar, and lemon zest until the mixture reaches a ribbon stage, where the whisk leaves a strong, three-dimensional shape. Remove the bowl from the mixer and fold in the all-purpose flour, almond flour, aniseeds, baking powder, and salt until just combined. Fold in the melted butter. Spoon the batter into a piping bag (do not cut an opening yet), tie the bag closed, and refrigerate the batter overnight.

Preheat the oven to 425°F (220°C). Spray a nonstick 12-cup madeleine pan with vegetable oil cooking spray.

Cut a ¼-inch (6-millimeter) opening straight across the tip of the pastry bag. Pipe the madeleine batter into each cavity of the pan, filling it nearly to the top. Immediately place the pan in the hot oven and bake for 10 to 11 minutes, or until the edges of the madeleines are golden and their top is puffed up. Remove from the oven and unmold immediately by inverting the pan onto a wire rack. Eat the same day.

Chestnut Madeleines

I love the smoky scent of chestnuts roasting in the streets that conveys the return of fall to New York City, and wanted to turn that scent into madeleines. The chestnuts increase the pastry's complexity, and a little more salt helps further enhance the overall flavor.

Makes 12 large madeleines

6 tablespoons (84 grams) unsalted butter

3 large eggs

⅓ cup (67 grams) granulated sugar

½ teaspoon (2 grams) pure vanilla extract

⅓ cup (45 grams) all-purpose flour

⅓ cup (50 grams) chestnut flour
(see Resources, page288)

¾ teaspoon (3 grams) baking powder

½ teaspoon (2 grams) fine sea salt

Vegetable oil cooking spray

Place the butter in a small saucepan over medium heat and let it melt. Remove from the heat and let it cool slightly.

In the bowl of an electric mixer fitted with the whisk attachment, whisk the eggs, sugar, and vanilla until the mixture reaches a ribbon stage, where the whisk leaves a strong, three-dimensional shape. Remove the bowl from the mixer and fold in the all-purpose flour, chestnut flour, baking powder, and salt until just combined. Fold in the melted butter. Spoon the batter into a piping bag (do not cut an opening yet), tie the bag closed, and refrigerate the batter overnight.

Preheat the oven to 425°F (220°C). Spray a nonstick 12-cup madeleine pan with vegetable oil cooking spray.

Cut a ¼-inch (6-millimeter) opening straight across the tip of the pastry bag. Pipe the madeleine batter into each cavity of the pan, filling it nearly to the top. Immediately place the pan in the hot oven and bake for 10 to 11 minutes, or until the edges of the madeleines are golden and their top is puffed up. Remove from the oven and unmold immediately by inverting the pan onto a wire rack. Eat the same day.

Pear-Rosemary Madeleines

I like to serve these madeleines at the end of a rich fall meal. The pear and rosemary flavor, with a little black pepper kick, make them both seasonal and not overly sweet.

Makes 16 large madeleines

6 tablespoons (84 grams) unsalted butter, divided

1 ripe pear (about 220 grams), peeled and cut into ¼-inch (6-millimeter) pieces

1 teaspoon (2 grams) finely chopped fresh rosemary

½ teaspoon (2 grams) fine sea salt, divided

¼ teaspoon (1 gram) freshly ground black pepper

2 large eggs

⅓ cup (67 grams) granulated sugar

½ cup (68 grams) all-purpose flour

⅓ cup (40 grams) almond flour

1 teaspoon (4 grams) baking powder

Vegetable oil cooking spray

Heat a medium sauté pan over medium heat. Place 2 tablespoons (28 grams) of the butter, the pear and rosemary, ¼ teaspoon (1 gram) of the salt, and the pepper in the pan and cook for about 8 minutes, stirring occasionally, until the pears begin to turn golden and translucent. Remove from the heat and set aside.

Place the remaining 4 tablespoons (56 grams) of butter in a small saucepan over medium heat and let it melt. Remove from the heat and let it cool slightly.

In the bowl of an electric mixer fitted with the whisk attachment, whisk the eggs and sugar until the mixture reaches a ribbon stage, where the whisk leaves a strong, three-dimensional shape. Remove the bowl from the mixer and fold in the all-purpose flour, almond flour, baking powder, and remaining ¼ teaspoon (1 gram) of salt until just combined. Fold in the melted butter and the pears. Spoon the batter into a piping bag (do not cut an opening yet), tie the bag closed, and refrigerate the batter overnight.

Preheat the oven to 425°F (220°C). Spray a nonstick 12-cup madeleine pan with vegetable oil cooking spray.

Cut a ½-inch (1.25-centimeter) opening straight across the tip of the pastry bag. Pipe the madeleine batter into each cavity of the pan, filling it nearly to the top. Immediately place the pan in the hot oven and bake for 10 to 11 minutes, or until the edges of the madeleines are golden and their top is puffed up. Refrigerate the extra batter while one batch bakes. Remove from the oven and unmold immediately by inverting the pan onto a wire rack. Repeat until the batter is used up. Eat the same day.

Banana–Brown Sugar Madeleines

Bananas take very well to the nuttiness of hazelnut flour. If you can't find hazelnut flour, grind your own in a food processor, being careful to not turn the hazelnuts into paste, or use almond flour.

Makes 16 large madeleines

6 tablespoons (84 grams) unsalted butter

2 large eggs

¼ packed cup (57 grams) dark brown sugar

1 ripe banana (about 100 grams in the peel), peeled and cut into ½-inch (1.25-centimeter) pieces

½ cup (68 grams) all-purpose flour

⅓ cup (40 grams) hazelnut flour

1 teaspoon (4 grams) baking powder

¼ teaspoon (1 gram) fine sea salt

Vegetable oil cooking spray

Place the butter in a small saucepan over medium heat and let it melt. Remove from the heat and let it cool slightly.

In the bowl of an electric mixer fitted with the whisk attachment, whisk the eggs and sugar until the mixture reaches a ribbon stage, where the whisk leaves a strong, three-dimensional shape. Remove the bowl from the mixer and fold in the bananas, all-purpose flour, hazelnut flour, baking powder, and salt until just combined. Fold in the melted butter. Spoon the batter into a piping bag (do not cut an opening yet), tie the bag closed, and refrigerate the batter overnight.

Preheat the oven to 425°F (220°C). Spray a nonstick 12-cup madeleine pan with vegetable oil cooking spray.

Cut a ½-inch (1.25-centimeter) opening straight across the tip of the pastry bag. Pipe the madeleine batter into each cavity of the pan, filling it nearly to the top. Immediately place the pan in the hot oven and bake for 10 to 11 minutes, or until the edges of the madeleines are golden and their top is puffed up. Refrigerate the extra batter while one batch bakes. Remove from the oven and unmold immediately by inverting the pan onto a wire rack. Repeat until the batter is used up. Eat the same day.

Fig-Fennel-Mascarpone Madeleines

These madeleines are inspired by cheese boards, where figs often are strewn around a selection of cheeses, since they complement so many of them. While mascarpone is rarely found on such cheese boards, its creamy texture works wonders in a madeleine batter. Fennel seeds add a subtle licorice-like note. Serve them at brunch, accompanied by extra mascarpone and fig jam to be spooned on the madeleines.

Makes 16 large madeleines

6 tablespoons (84 grams) unsalted butter, divided

6 ripe figs (about 220 grams), stemmed and cut into ¼-inch (6-millimeter) pieces

⅓ cup plus 2 tablespoons (91 grams) granulated sugar, divided

½ teaspoon (2 grams) fennel seeds

2 large eggs

½ cup (115 grams) mascarpone cheese

½ cup (68 grams) all-purpose flour

⅓ cup (40 grams) almond flour

1 teaspoon (4 grams) baking powder

¼ teaspoon (1 gram) fine sea salt

Vegetable oil cooking spray

Heat a medium sauté pan over medium heat. Place 2 tablespoons (28 grams) of the butter, the figs, 2 tablespoons (28 grams) of the sugar, and the fennel seeds in the pan and cook for 3 minutes, stirring carefully. Remove from the heat and set aside.

Place the remaining 4 tablespoons (56 grams) of butter in a small saucepan over medium heat and let it melt. Remove from the heat and let it cool slightly.

In the bowl of an electric mixer fitted with the whisk attachment, whisk the eggs and remaining ⅓ cup (67 grams) of the sugar until the mixture reaches a ribbon stage, where the whisk leaves a strong, three-dimensional shape.

Whisk a little bit of the egg mixture into the mascarpone to loosen it, then add the mascarpone to the mixing bowl and whisk until just combined.

Remove the bowl from the mixer and fold in the all-purpose flour, almond flour, baking powder, and salt until just combined. Fold in the melted butter and the figs. Spoon the batter in a piping bag (do not cut an opening yet), tie the bag closed, and refrigerate the batter overnight.

Preheat the oven to 425°F (220°C). Spray a nonstick 12-cup madeleine pan with vegetable oil cooking spray.

Cut a ½-inch (1.25-centimeter) opening straight across the tip of the pastry bag. Pipe the madeleine batter in each cavity of the pan, filling it nearly to the top. Immediately place the pan in the hot oven and bake for 10 to 11 minutes, or until the edges of the madeleines are golden and their top is puffed up. Refrigerate the extra batter while one batch bakes. Remove from the oven and unmold immediately by inverting the pan onto a wire rack. Repeat until the batter is used up. Eat the same day.

Chocolate-Prune Tea Cakes

Tea Cakes

ALMOND-BRANDIED CHERRY TEA CAKES

RASPBERRY-VANILLA TEA CAKES

ORANGE BLOSSOM TEA CAKES

CHOCOLATE-PRUNE TEA CAKES

TEA CAKES ARE SIMILAR TO FINANCIERS AND MADELEINES IN THAT THEY ARE small, moist, and easy to make, and can take on a wide range of flavors. The batter does not need to rest overnight and contains melted butter rather than beurre noisette. They also freeze well and can be baked in a variety of shapes. In short, they are ideal when you need to get something sweet on the table, and fast. It's the type of treat your guests will admire, while never guessing how little work they require. As with financiers, you can bake them in a variety of (small) molds, keeping in mind that the yield might accordingly vary. As standard, use a mini-muffin pan (mine measures 1¾ inches/4.5 centimeters at the top and 1¼ inches/3 centimeters at the bottom), or use these recipes as an excuse to pick up silicone molds with similarly small cavities.

Almond-Brandied Cherry Tea Cakes

The first bite-size tea cakes I made were while training at Le Bernardin with chef Hervé Poussot. There, they were called "soufflé" cakes. I've since continued to toy with the recipe, arriving at this one. Feel free to do the same and vary the fruits used. The cherries here only macerate for a day; they will not be as strongly flavored as those steeping in brandy for months, but the difference is small compared with the time gained. Of course, use fruits that have marinated longer if you have them, cutting larger fruits into ½-inch (1.25-centimeter) pieces so that they fit the molds.

Makes 18 to 24 (1¾-inch/4.5-centimeter) cakes

2 tablespoons (28 grams) unsalted butter

¾ cup (81 grams) almond flour

½ cup (100 grams) granulated sugar

3 large eggs

2 tablespoons (30 grams) heavy whipping cream

¼ cup (34 grams) all-purpose flour

¼ teaspoon (1 gram) fine sea salt

18 to 24 brandied cherries, drained (recipe follows)

1 teaspoon (5 grams) confectioners' sugar for dusting

Preheat the oven to 350°F (175°C) and line mini-muffin pans (or other similarly sized molds) with aluminum foil or paper baking cups.

Melt the butter in a small saucepan over low heat and set aside.

In the bowl of an electric mixer fitted with the paddle attachment, mix together the almond flour, granulated sugar, and eggs on medium speed until the mixture is smooth. Drizzle in the melted butter and cream, then mix in the all-purpose flour and salt until just combined, about 30 seconds.

Spoon or pipe the batter two thirds of the way into the lined cups. Place a brandied cherry at the center of each cake and bake until the centers have risen and the cakes' edges are slightly colored but still soft, about 10 minutes. Transfer the cups to a wire rack and let cool completely. Wrapped tightly in plastic wrap, they will keep for 2 weeks in the refrigerator and 1 month in the freezer.

Just before serving, place the confectioners' sugar in a small fine-mesh sieve and gently tap the sieve over the tea cakes to dust them with the sugar.

BRANDIED CHERRIES

You can use store-bought Morello cherries in brandy for this recipe, but it's easy enough to make your own brandied cherries. All you need is 24 hours (of course, you can let them macerate for a longer period of time, if you wish).

Makes ⅓ cup (50 grams)

⅓ cup (50 grams) fresh sweet or sour red or white cherries

2 ounces (60 grams) brandy (substitute kirsch or Grand Marnier)

Place the cherries and brandy in a small bowl or container, cover, and let marinate overnight in the refrigerator. Drain the cherries well before using them in tea cakes, saving the brandy for another project—or for a drink.

Raspberry-Vanilla Tea Cakes

Freeze-dried fruits have become widely available (Trader Joe's has a large selection, as do most large supermarkets, not to mention specialty stores) and are perfect for this recipe, since fresh or frozen raspberries contain too much water and would make for too liquid a batter. Try this recipe with other freeze-dried fruits, such as mangoes, pineapples, or blueberries.

Makes 18 to 24
(1¾-inch/4.5-centimeter) cakes

1 vanilla bean

2 tablespoons (28 grams) unsalted butter

¾ cup (81 grams) almond flour

½ cup (100 grams) granulated sugar

3 large eggs

¼ packed teaspoon (1 gram) finely grated lemon zest (from ¼ lemon)

2 tablespoons (30 grams) heavy whipping cream

1 teaspoon (4 grams) pure vanilla extract

¼ cup (34 grams) all-purpose flour

½ cup (7.5 grams) freeze-dried raspberries, cut into ¼-inch (6-millimeter) pieces (see Resources, page 288)

¼ teaspoon (1 gram) fine sea salt

1 teaspoon (5 grams) confectioners' sugar for dusting

Preheat the oven to 350°F (175°C) and line mini muffin pans (or other similarly sized molds) with aluminum foil or paper cups.

Split the vanilla bean lengthwise and scrape out the seeds with the back of a paring knife. Place the butter, vanilla seeds, and vanilla bean in a small saucepan over low heat, cook until the butter is melted, and set aside.

In the bowl of an electric mixer fitted with the paddle attachment, mix together the almond flour, granulated sugar, eggs, and lemon zest on medium speed until the mixture is smooth. Drizzle in the melted butter (remove the vanilla bean first), cream, and vanilla, then mix in the all-purpose flour, raspberries, and salt until just combined, about 30 seconds.

Spoon or pipe the batter two thirds of the way into the lined cups and bake until the centers have risen and the cakes' edges are slightly colored but still soft, about 10 minutes. Transfer the cups to a wire rack and let cool completely. Wrapped tightly in plastic wrap, they will keep for 2 weeks in the refrigerator and 1 month in the freezer.

Just before serving, place the confectioners' sugar in a small fine-mesh sieve and gently tap the sieve over the tea cakes to dust them with the sugar.

Variation

ORANGE BLOSSOM TEA CAKES

Omit the raspberries, lemon zest, vanilla bean, and vanilla. Add 1 tablespoon (20 grams) of orange blossom water and the finely grated zest of ½ orange (4 grams) with the eggs.

Chocolate-Prune Tea Cakes

I first came across the intriguing combination of chocolate and prune in a David Lebovitz macaron recipe. They go together brilliantly, with depth and complexity. Here, the prunes are marinated in dark rum, but feel free to use plum brandy or bourbon if you prefer.

Makes 18 to 24
(1¾-inch/4.5-centimeter) cakes

½ cup (83 grams) prunes, cut into ½-inch (1.25-centimeter) pieces

2 tablespoons (30 grams) dark rum

2 tablespoons (28 grams) unsalted butter

4 ounces (113 grams) semisweet chocolate, finely chopped (about ¾ cup chopped)

¾ cup (81 grams) almond flour

½ cup (100 grams) granulated sugar

3 large eggs

¼ cup (34 grams) all-purpose flour

¼ teaspoon (1 gram) fine sea salt

Place the cut prunes and rum in a small bowl or container and let marinate at room temperature for 30 minutes.

Preheat the oven to 350°F (175°C) and line mini muffin pans (or other similarly sized molds) with aluminum foil or paper baking cups.

Melt the butter in a small saucepan over medium-low heat, then remove from the heat and add the chocolate pieces, shaking the pan so that the chocolate is completely submerged. Let the mixture sit for 1 minute, then whisk from the center until it is smooth and the chocolate is completely melted.

In the bowl of an electric mixer fitted with the paddle attachment, mix together the almond flour, granulated sugar, and eggs on medium speed until the mixture is smooth. Mix in the melted chocolate mixture until smooth, then mix in the all-purpose flour and salt until just combined, about 30 seconds.

Spoon or pipe the batter two thirds of the way into the lined cups and bake until the centers have risen and the cakes' edges are slightly colored but still soft, about 10 minutes. Transfer the cups to a wire rack and let cool completely. Wrapped tightly in plastic wrap, they will keep for 2 weeks in the refrigerator and 1 month in the freezer.

Raspberry-Tarragon Savarins

SAVARINS

I FIRST LEARNED HOW TO BAKE SAVARINS WHILE IN PASTRY SCHOOL AT L'ACADÉMIE de Cuisine in Maryland and later made them for every dessert buffet at the Rainbow Room; to say they are a classic French dessert is an understatement. Individually sized versions are widely available in pastry shops in France and Switzerland, along with baba au rhum, savarin's cousin, which is typically baked in a tall and narrow mold rather than a low, wide one—but the two shapes and names are more and more used interchangeably, I find, whether or not it's correct to do so. The neutral yeast dough is not particularly sweet and will take on the characteristics of any syrup in which you soak it. Although savarins are classically made with a rum syrup, I offer here a variety of other flavors as a launching pad for your own creative efforts. I bake them a little longer and at a lower heat than other pastry chefs, because doing so dries them out more and they absorb the syrup more easily; this allows you to soak them the same day they are made. They are served with crème chantilly (see page 65) but you can also use store-bought crème fraîche, either as is for a slightly tarter flavor, or with a little vanilla sugar (see page 21) stirred in.

Base Savarin Recipe

You can use silicone or tin savarin molds, which are both available in specialty baking stores and online. You can also use this recipe with baba molds. The final yield of the recipe will vary depending on the size of mold you use (the metal molds tend to be larger than the silicone ones). I use an 18-cavity silicone mold.

Makes 36 (1½-inch/4-centimeter)
or 12 (2¾-inch/7-centimeter) savarins

¼ cup (58 grams) milk

1 scant tablespoon (7 grams) Red Star SAF instant yeast
(see Resources, page 288)

1 cup (135 grams) all-purpose flour

2 large eggs

1 teaspoon (4 grams) pure vanilla extract

¼ teaspoon (1 gram) fine sea salt

½ packed teaspoon (2 grams) finely grated orange zest (from ¼ orange)

½ packed teaspoon (2 grams) finely grated lemon zest (from ½ lemon)

4 tablespoons (56 grams) unsalted butter, at room temperature,
cut into 1-inch (2.5-centimeter) pieces

1 tablespoon (14 grams) unsalted butter for the molds

Vegetable oil cooking spray

Place the milk in the bowl of an electric mixer. Whisk in the yeast until dissolved. Set the mixer with the paddle attachment, then add the flour, eggs, vanilla, salt, and orange and lemon zest and mix on medium speed for 2 minutes to combine. Turn off the mixer, change to the dough hook attachment, then with the mixer running on low speed, knead until the dough is smooth, shiny, and elastic and pulls away from the sides of the bowl, about 5 minutes. With the mixer running at its lowest speed, slowly add the butter pieces to the dough, adding the next when the last one is incorporated, until all the butter is incorporated. It will take about 15 minutes.

Remove the bowl from the mixer, cover the top with plastic wrap, and set the bowl in a warm area for 1 hour.

Grease the savarin molds with the tablespoon (14 grams) of butter.

Once the dough has risen, stir it with a spatula to recombine it, then spoon the dough into a piping bag fitted with a ¼-inch (6-millimeter) round tip (alternatively, cut a ¼-inch opening in the bag). Pipe a ring of batter into the molds, filling them only halfway up. Spray plastic wrap with vegetable oil cooking spray and loosely cover the molds with the plastic so that the dough doesn't dry up. Place in a warm spot until the dough doubles in size and fills the molds to the top, about 45 minutes.

Preheat the oven to 325°F (160°C).

Bake the savarins for 35 minutes, rotating halfway through if they are browning too much on one side. Remove from the oven and let cool 5 minutes. Carefully remove the savarins from the molds, invert the molds, and set the savarins on top of the molds to cool. You can store them in an airtight container at room temperature for up to 24 hours if you don't want to soak them right away. Wrapped tightly in plastic wrap, they will keep in the freezer for up to 2 months.

To prepare the savarins to soak up the syrup in the recipes that follow, poke both sides carefully and evenly with a bamboo skewer.

Bring the syrup to a boil over medium-high heat, then remove from the heat. Place half of the savarins in the saucepan and let them soak for 5 minutes. With a slotted spoon, flip them and let them soak 10 minutes on that side. Use a slotted spoon to transfer them to a serving platter or storage container. Bring the syrup back to a boil and repeat the procedure until all the savarins are soaked.

Pour any remaining syrup evenly over and around the savarins. Chill for 1 hour before serving with Vanilla Crème Chantilly (recipe follows) and a fruit topping.

VANILLA CRÈME CHANTILLY

Homemade chantilly has a lightness and uniquely tangy flavor that takes desserts to heights a simple whipped cream won't reach. It's the traditional accompaniment of many a French dessert, including ice-cream sundaes and cakes. If you prefer or are short on time, you can also spoon store-bought crème fraîche (which is what you are essentially making before adding the vanilla sugar) on top of the savarins.

Makes about 1 cup, enough for 36 (1½-inch/4-centimeter) or 12 (2¾-inch/7-centimeter) savarins

1 cup (240 grams) heavy whipping cream

1 tablespoon (15 grams) natural, plain yogurt with active cultures

1 tablespoon (15 grams) buttermilk

½ vanilla bean

1 tablespoon (12 grams) granulated sugar

Place the cream, yogurt, and buttermilk in a stainless-steel bowl and stir them to combine for 15 seconds. Cover the bowl with plastic wrap and leave the mixture out at room temperature (about 75°F/24°C) for 24 hours.

Split the vanilla bean lengthwise and scrape out the seeds with the back of a paring knife into the sugar. Rub the bean into the sugar to scrape out more vanilla seeds and thoroughly stir the sugar to make sure the vanilla is homogenously dispersed. Reserve the bean for another use. Stir the vanilla sugar into the cream mixture, and refrigerate before serving. It will keep, covered and refrigerated, for up to 1 week.

Raspberry-Tarragon Savarins

Famed French pastry chef Philippe Conticini makes savarins with a peach syrup, which inspired this raspberry version. Tarragon is also a quintessential French herb; this syrup is a great way to use extra when you've bought some for a savory dish.

Makes about 4 cups (1 kilogram) of syrup, enough for 36 (1½-inch/4-centimeter) or 12 (2¾-inch/7-centimeter) savarins

3 cups (600 grams) granulated sugar

2 cups (460 grams) water

2 dry half-pints (340 grams total) fresh raspberries, divided

2 tablespoons (10 grams) fresh tarragon leaves

2 tablespoons (30 grams) Framboise

1 recipe Savarins (page 63)

1 recipe Vanilla Crème Chantilly (page 65)

Place the sugar in a medium saucepan. Pour the water around the edges of the pan and at the center of the sugar. Bring the sugar to a boil over medium heat, stirring only as needed to help the sugar dissolve and without touching the edges of the pot. When the sugar is dissolved, stir in ½ dry pint (170 grams) of the raspberries and the tarragon. Once the syrup has boiled, remove it from the heat and strain the syrup into a bowl with a fine-mesh sieve or a chinois, gently pressing it with a spatula to make sure you get everything. Stir in the Framboise. If using right away, pour the syrup back into the saucepan and return to the stove over low heat. The syrup will keep, covered and refrigerated, for up to 2 days.

Soak the savarins in the syrup as described on page 64. Spoon or pipe a dollop of crème chantilly in the center of each savarin and top with the remaining dry half-pint (170 grams) of raspberries.

Caramelized Banana–Rum Savarins

Anne has fond memories of *bananes flambées* from her childhood's summers, when bananas wrapped in aluminum foil were placed to cook on the dying embers of charcoals on the grill after a roast, to be then flambéed with a bit of rum or Grand Marnier (the alcohol cooked off, not to worry). Bananas Foster, popularized in New Orleans, is the restaurant equivalent, when bananas are sautéed and flambéed table side. These savarins capture the same great flavors.

Makes 4 cups (1 kilogram) of syrup, enough for
36 (1½-inch/4-centimeter) or 12 (2¾-inch/7-centimeter) savarins

2 bananas (about 200 grams in the peel),
peeled and cut into ¼-inch (6-millimeter) pieces

2 tablespoons (30 grams) freshly squeezed
and strained orange juice (from ¼ orange)

3 cups (600 grams) granulated sugar

1 teaspoon (5 grams) freshly squeezed
and strained lemon juice (from ⅛ lemon)

2 cups (460 grams) water, divided

1 tablespoon (15 grams) dark rum

1 recipe Savarins (page 63)

1 recipe Vanilla Crème Chantilly (page 65)

In a medium bowl, gently toss the banana pieces with the orange juice to coat them.

Place the sugar in a medium saucepan and stir in the lemon juice. Pour 1 cup (230 grams) of the water around the edges of the pan and cook the sugar over medium heat until it turns a clear, dark amber color (see box, below).

While the syrup is cooking, boil the remaining 1 cup (230 grams) of water in a small saucepan over high heat. Once the syrup has reached the proper color, remove it from the heat and, holding the pot at arm's length to avoid splatters, quickly pour the hot water into the syrup. Stir with a heat-resistant spatula to dissolve the water into syrup. Stir in the rum. Pour the syrup over the bananas, stir gently to fully coat the bananas in the syrup, and let cool for 30 minutes.

Drain the syrup back into the pan and reserve the banana pieces separately.

Soak the savarins in the syrup as described on page 64. Spoon or pipe a dollop of crème chantilly in the center of each savarin and top with a spoonful of bananas.

CARAMELIZATION

Be careful to cook the sugar syrup all the way to caramel or the diluted syrup will just taste like sugar. Don't just look at the color in the pot, which can be deceiving. Dip a heat-resistant spatula in the caramel and let it drip back into the pot to see its real color. It should be a clear, dark amber and should smell like caramel. I just eyeball the syrup, but you could clip a calibrated thermometer onto the saucepan and cook the caramel to 330°F (166°C).

Blueberry-Lemongrass Savarins

Lemongrass has a slight herbaceous flavor that I find works well with blueberries, which appear here in the form of a compote. We used to make a dessert at Windows on the World with a similar compote in a crisp spring roll. These are fruity, summery savarins that can also be made with blackberries—but strain the compote to get rid of half the seeds, in that case.

Makes about 4 cups (1 kilogram) of syrup and 1 pint (400 grams) of compote, enough for 36 (1½-inch/4-centimeter) or 12 (2¾-inch/7-centimeter) savarins

LEMONGRASS SYRUP

6 stalks lemongrass

3 cups (600 grams) granulated sugar

2 cups (460 grams) water

16 black peppercorns

BLUEBERRY COMPOTE

½ vanilla bean

½ cup (100 grams) granulated sugar

Reserved center pieces from 6 stalks lemongrass

1 dry pint (300 grams) fresh blueberries

1 small pinch of fleur de sel

1 recipe Savarins (page 63)

1 recipe Vanilla Crème Chantilly (page 65)

MAKE THE LEMONGRASS SYRUP: With a chef's knife, trim off the dry tops and bottoms of the lemongrass stalks. Place the stalks on a flat surface and firmly smash the bulb of each with a rolling pin. The very center of the bulb, about 1 to 2 inches (2.5 to 5 centimeters) long, is flexible and edible. Reserve these center pieces and cut the remaining stalks into 1-inch (2.5-centimeter) pieces.

Place the sugar in a medium saucepan. Pour the water around the edges of the pan and at the center of the sugar. Add the lemongrass stalk pieces and the peppercorns. Bring the sugar to a boil over medium heat, stirring only as needed to help the sugar dissolve and without touching the edges of the pot. Once the mixture has boiled, remove it from the heat and let it steep for 30 minutes.

MAKE THE BLUEBERRY COMPOTE: Split the vanilla bean lengthwise and scrape out the seeds with the back of a paring knife into the sugar. Rub the bean into the sugar to scrape out more vanilla seeds and thoroughly stir the sugar to make sure the vanilla is homogenously dispersed. Reserve the bean for another use.

Very finely cut the reserved soft lemongrass centers into pieces that measure about 1⁄16 of an inch (1.5 millimeters).

Place enough ice cubes in a bowl to fill it a quarter of the way up. Pour just enough water to get the ice cubes to loosely float, not adding more than necessary or the ice cubes will melt.

Heat the vanilla sugar, center lemongrass pieces, and blueberries in a medium saucepan over medium heat, stirring constantly with a heat-resistant spatula to coat the blueberries with the sugar. Cook until the mixture begins to thicken and becomes jellylike, about 10 minutes. Remove from the heat, stir in the fleur de sel, and cool the pan over the ice-water bath.

When the lemongrass syrup is finished steeping, strain the syrup into a bowl with a fine-mesh sieve or a chinois, gently pressing it with a spatula to make sure you get everything. If using right away to soak the savarins, reboil the syrup in a saucepan. The syrup will keep, covered and refrigerated, for up to 2 days.

Soak the savarins in the lemongrass syrup as described on page 64. Spoon a dollop of blueberry compote in the center of each savarin. Top with a dollop of crème chantilly.

Lychee-Ginger-Anise Savarins

I love buying fresh lychees when they are in season and sold on street corners in Chinatown (or at a supermarket), peeling away their rough but thin skin and digging into their juicy flesh. While fresh lychees are great to eat as is, I tend to buy lots of them at once and come up with desserts that vary things up a bit—these savarins do just that. The anise and ginger add heat to the syrup. If using canned lychees, save the can's syrup when you drain them and enjoy it with seltzer water.

Makes 4 cups (1 kilogram) of syrup, enough for
36 (1½-inch/4-centimeter) or 12 (2¾-inch/7-centimeter) savarins

1 pound (454 grams) fresh lychees, peeled and seeded, or 1 (20-ounce [567-gram]) can, drained

1 tablespoon (25 grams, about 6 big pieces) crystalized ginger

3 cups (600 grams) granulated sugar

2 cups (460 grams) water

12 star anise

1 recipe Savarins (page 63)

1 recipe Vanilla Crème Chantilly (page 65)

Cut the lychees into ¼-inch (6-millimeter) pieces, to make about 1 cup (227 grams). Cut the ginger into ¼-inch pieces and stir it into the lychees.

Place the sugar in a medium saucepan. Pour the water around the edges of the pan and at the center of the sugar. Add the star anise. Bring the sugar to a boil over medium heat, stirring only as needed to help the sugar dissolve and without touching the edges of the pot. Once the mixture has boiled, remove it from the heat, stir in the lychee and ginger pieces, and let it steep for 1 hour. Strain the syrup into a bowl with a fine-mesh sieve or a chinois, gently pressing it with a spatula to make sure you get everything. Reserve the lychee and ginger pieces in a separate container.

Soak the savarins in the syrup as described on page 64. Spoon a dollop of crème chantilly in the center of each savarin and top with a spoonful of lychees and ginger.

Lapsang Souchong Cannelés

Cannelés

ARMAGNAC-VANILLA CANNELÉS

ST-GERMAIN CANNELÉS

POIRE WILLIAMS CANNELÉS

COCONUT-LIME CANNELÉS

LAPSANG SOUCHONG CANNELÉS

I HAVE MANY FAVORITE PASTRIES—IT'S A PROFESSIONAL MUST—BUT CANNELÉS RANK very high among them. They are originally from Bordeaux but are found throughout France, and increasingly throughout the United States, too, whether in pastry shops or, in mini sizes, on mignardise trays in restaurants. Cannelés are baked in a distinctive fluted mold that is brushed with melted beeswax. In addition to their shape, their signature elements are a crispy dark crust and moist interior that is almost a hybrid between cake and custard. You can make them in silicone molds, but if you consider yourself a serious cannelé aficionado, invest in copper or stainless-steel molds. Making cannelé batter is easy and takes little actual time, but the overall process requires a bit of planning, since the molds need to be readied and the batter needs to chill overnight. The size of cannelé molds varies widely from one maker to another. You'll get sixteen small cannelés with the recipes that follow if you use a 1-ounce (28-gram)-cavity silicone mold. Fill the molds three quarters of the way up, since the cannelés will expand a bit while baking. If you have batter left over while baking a batch, keep it in the refrigerator until the first batch is done.

SEASONING CANNELÉ MOLDS

Before you use new, clean copper or stainless-steel cannelé molds, you'll need to season them with beeswax, which you can find at the stand of a beekeeper at a farmers' market or online. The best beeswax will have a deep amber color. Preheat the oven to 350°F (175°C). Melt the beeswax over a double boiler (see page 18) or in a microwave. With a dry pastry brush, thoroughly and evenly brush the wax into the molds. Arrange the molds on a baking sheet and place them in the oven for 1 hour.

Line a baking sheet with parchment paper, place a rack on the sheet, and carefully flip the hot molds onto the rack. Bake the molds for another 15 minutes, then turn off the oven and leave the molds in there until they are completely cooled. Store them until ready to use.

When your molds are seasoned, you can use vegetable oil cooking spray before filling them with the batter.

After baking cannelés in seasoned molds, don't wash the molds, but rub them clean with a dry towel.

Armagnac-Vanilla Cannelés

While rum is often used in cannelés, I love the depth of flavor that Armagnac provides. Because it is also less common, it makes for a more surprising taste, one that those eating these cannelés might not be able to immediately identify.

Makes 16 (1 x 1¼-inch/2.5 x 3-centimeter) cannelés

½ cup (90 grams) confectioners' sugar

½ vanilla bean

½ cup (68 grams) all-purpose flour

⅛ teaspoon (0.7 gram) fine sea salt

1 cup (230 grams) milk

4 tablespoons (56 grams) unsalted butter, divided

1 large egg

1 large egg yolk

2 tablespoons (30 grams) Armagnac

¼ cup (10 grams) grated beeswax
(see Resources, page 288)

Sift the sugar into a medium bowl. Split the vanilla bean lengthwise and scrape out the seeds with the back of a paring knife into the sugar. Rub the bean into the sugar to scrape out more vanilla seeds. Mix in the flour and salt, and set aside.

Place the scraped vanilla bean in a small saucepan over medium-high heat, add the milk and 2 tablespoons (28 grams) of the butter, and bring to a boil. Turn off the heat and let the mixture steep and cool slightly for 15 minutes. Remove the vanilla bean.

In a large bowl, whisk the egg and yolk to combine them, then whisk in the warm milk and the Armagnac. Whisk in the flour mixture in three batches, doing so gently until the ingredients are just combined. Strain the batter through a fine-mesh sieve or a chinois into another bowl or container, cover, and refrigerate for 24 to 36 hours.

Prepare your copper or stainless-steel cannelés molds by melting the beeswax and remaining 2 tablespoons (28 grams) of butter in the microwave for about 1 minute. Brush the molds evenly and thoroughly with a 1-inch (2.5-centimeter)-wide pastry brush. Freeze the molds overnight. Preparing the molds this way every time helps the texture of the finished cannelés and is worth the effort.

If using a silicone mold, coat it with vegetable oil cooking spray and use immediately.

Preheat the oven to 425°F (220°C) and arrange the molds on a baking sheet.

Gently stir the batter to recombine any settled solids. Pour the batter into a piping bag without a tip, and cut a ⅛-inch (3-millimeter) opening in the bag, or pour it into a cup with a spout, such as a measuring cup, and then pipe or pour the batter into the prepared molds, filling them only three quarters of the way up. Bake for 20 minutes, then lower the heat to 400°F (200°C) and bake for 20 additional minutes. Rotate the pans every 10 minutes, three times total.

Remove the pans from the oven and let the cannelés cool in them for 5 minutes, then unmold from the pan and place them on a wire rack to cool completely. If a cannelé is stuck, use a bamboo skewer to help release it. Store in an airtight container at room temperature for up to 3 days.

Variation:

ST-GERMAIN CANNELÉS

Omit the vanilla bean. Substitute ¼ cup (60 grams) of St-Germain for the Armagnac and omit 1 tablespoon (12 grams) of milk.

Variation

POIRE WILLIAMS CANNELÉS

Substitute 3 tablespoons (45 grams) Poire Williams eau de vie for the Armagnac.

Coconut-Lime Cannelés

I often substitute coconut milk for cow's milk, especially if someone on my guest list is lactose intolerant. The flavor makes for a modern cannelé, with just a hint of lime to complement the coconut.

Makes 16
(1 x 1¼-inch/2.5 x 3-centimeter) cannelés

½ packed cup (110 grams) dark brown sugar

½ cup (68 grams) all-purpose flour

⅛ teaspoon (0.7 gram) fine sea salt

1 cup (250 grams) canned coconut milk

½ teaspoon (2 grams) finely grated lime zest

¼ teaspoon (0.75 gram) ground ginger

4 tablespoons (56 grams)
unsalted butter, divided

1 large egg

1 large egg yolk

¼ cup (10 grams) grated beeswax
(see Resources, page 288)

Place the sugar in a medium bowl. Mix in the flour and salt, and set aside.

Place the coconut milk, lime zest, ginger, and 2 tablespoons (28 grams) of the butter in a small saucepan over medium-high heat, and bring to a boil. Turn off the heat and let the mixture steep and cool slightly for 5 minutes.

In a large bowl, whisk the egg and yolk to combine them, then whisk in the warm coconut milk. Whisk in the flour mixture in three batches, doing so gently until the ingredients are just combined. Strain the batter through a fine-mesh sieve or a chinois into another bowl or container, cover, and refrigerate for 24 to 36 hours.

Prepare your copper or stainless-steel cannelés molds by melting the beeswax and remaining 2 tablespoons (28 grams) of butter in the microwave for about 1 minute. Brush the molds evenly and thoroughly with a 1-inch (2.5-centimeter)-wide pastry brush. Freeze the molds overnight. Preparing the molds this way every time helps the texture of the finished cannelés and is worth the effort.

If using a silicone mold, coat it with vegetable oil cooking spray and use immediately.

Preheat the oven to 425°F (220°C) and arrange the molds on a baking sheet.

Gently stir the batter to recombine any settled solids. Pour the batter into a piping bag without a tip, and cut a ⅛-inch (3-millimeter) opening in the bag, or pour it into a cup with a spout, such as a measuring cup, and then pipe or pour the batter into the prepared molds, filling them only three quarters of the way up. Bake for 20 minutes, then reduce the heat to 400°F (200°C) and bake for 20 additional minutes. Rotate the pans every 10 minutes, three times total.

Remove the pans from the oven and let the cannelés cool in them for 5 minutes, then unmold from the pan and place them on a wire rack to cool completely. If a cannelé is stuck, use a bamboo skewer to help release it. Store in an airtight container at room temperature for up to 3 days.

Lapsang Souchong Cannelés

Lapsang Souchong is one of my most favorite teas to have at afternoon tea in Paris. The tea's subtle smokiness infuses nicely into milk, so it works particularly well in this eggy, dairy-based batter.

Makes 16
(1 x 1¼-inch/2.5 x 3-centimeter) cannelés

½ cup (90 grams) confectioners' sugar

½ cup (68 grams) all-purpose flour

⅛ teaspoon (0.7 gram) fine sea salt

1 cup (230 grams) milk

4 tablespoons (56 grams)
unsalted butter, divided

1 tablespoon (4 grams) Lapsang Souchong tea

1 large egg

1 large egg yolk

¼ cup (10 grams) grated beeswax
(see Resources, page 288)

Sift the sugar into a medium bowl. Mix in the flour and salt, and set aside.

Place the milk and 2 tablespoons (28 grams) of the butter in a small saucepan over medium-high heat. At the boil, add the tea and let steep for 6 minutes. Stir, and thoroughly press the mixture through a sieve. Let cool slightly for 5 minutes.

In a large bowl, whisk the egg and yolk to combine them, then whisk in the warm milky tea. Whisk in the flour mixture in three batches, doing so gently until the ingredients are just combined. Strain the batter through a fine-mesh sieve or a chinois into another bowl or a reusable container, cover, and refrigerate for 24 to 36 hours.

Prepare your copper or stainless-steel cannelés molds by melting the beeswax and remaining 2 tablespoons (28 grams) of butter in the microwave for about 1 minute. Brush the molds evenly and thoroughly with a 1-inch (2.5-centimeter)-wide pastry brush. Freeze the molds overnight. Preparing the molds this way every time helps the texture of the finished cannelés and is worth the effort.

If using a silicone mold, coat it with vegetable oil cooking spray and use immediately.

Preheat the oven to 425°F (220°C) and arrange the molds on a baking sheet.

Gently stir the batter to recombine any settled solids. Pour the batter into a piping bag without a tip, and cut a ⅛-inch (3-millimeter) opening in the bag, or pour it into a cup with a spout, such as a measuring cup, and then pipe or pour the batter into the prepared molds, filling them only three quarters of the way up. Bake for 20 minutes, then reduce the heat to 400°F (200°C) and bake for 20 additional minutes. Rotate the pans every 10 minutes, three times total.

Remove the pans from the oven and let the cannelés cool in them for 5 minutes, then unmold from the pan and place them on a wire rack to cool completely. If a cannelé is stuck, use a bamboo skewer to help release it. Store in an airtight container at room temperature for up to 3 days.

Grapefruit and Cantaloupe Calissons

CALISSONS

GRAPEFRUIT AND CANTALOUPE CALISSONS

ORANGE BLOSSOM CALISSONS

PECAN-CINNAMON CALISSONS

HAZELNUT–CACAO NIB CALISSONS

CALISSONS ARE VERY FRENCH AND, STRANGELY SINCE THEY ARE SUCH GREAT treats, rarely found outside of France (but thankfully, Anne regularly receives shipments). They feature an almond-based dough that requires no baking, flavored with orange blossom water and glazed in white or a variety of pastel colors. Both the dough and the glaze are simple to prepare. The newer your food processor blade, the smoother the paste will be and the easier it will be to roll out the dough, but even if the dough isn't completely smooth, the calissons will taste marvelous paired with a variety of flavors and glazes. The only tricky part is to cut them in equal diamond shapes, but even there, imperfect shapes will have no bearing on their flavor. Roll or pat out the dough into a rectangle about

11 x 4 inches (28 x 10 centimeters), about ⅓ inch (8.5 millimeters) thick, and cut the dough into diamonds that are about ¾ inch (2 centimeters) on each side (see page 90 for a diagram, or you can buy a football-shaped cookie cutter, which will give you the slightly rounded edges characteristic of calissons; see Resources, page 288). Look for wafer paper online. It is available in rice (which will keep the calissons gluten-free) or wheat. Do not buy spring roll wrappers, which, while more readily available, are not the correct type of base.

Grapefruit and Cantaloupe Calissons

Calissons traditionally are often made with candied melon. Here, I use grapefruit and cantaloupe instead. You can use any store-bought candied fruits instead of making your own, but it's easy enough to do it yourself.

Makes about 20 (¾-inch/2-centimeter) calissons

1¼ cups (135 grams) almond flour

⅔ cup (100 grams) confectioners' sugar, plus more for assembly

⅛ teaspoon (1 gram) fine sea salt

1 tablespoon (25 grams) apricot preserves

⅓ cup (55 grams) grapefruit confit (recipe follows), drained well

⅓ cup (60 grams) candied cantaloupe (recipe follows), drained well

2 (11 x 8½-inch/28 x 22-centimeter) sheets wafer paper (see Resources, page 288)

Orange Blossom Glaze (recipe follows)

Place the almond flour, sugar, salt, and apricot preserves in the bowl of a food processor and pulse about 25 times, until a smooth paste forms. Stop and scrape the sides of the bowl every 5 pulses to ensure that all the ingredients are mixing smoothly. Add the grapefruit confit and candied cantaloupe and pulse them in, 5 pulses more. You should be able to press the dough into a ball with your hands.

Place one sheet of the wafer paper on waxed or parchment paper, shiny side up. Place half of the dough on the wafer paper, sprinkle it with confectioners' sugar to prevent the rolling pin from sticking, and roll it out into a rectangle about 11 x 4 inches (28 x 10 centimeters) and ⅓ inch (8.5 millimeters) thick. Repeat the process with the second half of the dough.

With a calisson or diamond cookie cutter (see Resources, page 288), a chef's knife, or a sharp pizza cutter, cut the dough into diamonds. If using a knife or pizza cutter, use a ruler to cut ¾-inch (2-centimeter)-wide strips parallel to each other. Then place the ruler at the bottom left of the dough on a 45-degree angle. Measure 1-inch (2.5-centimeter)-wide strips parallel to each other, and then the cut diamond shapes that form. Use the diagram below as a guide.

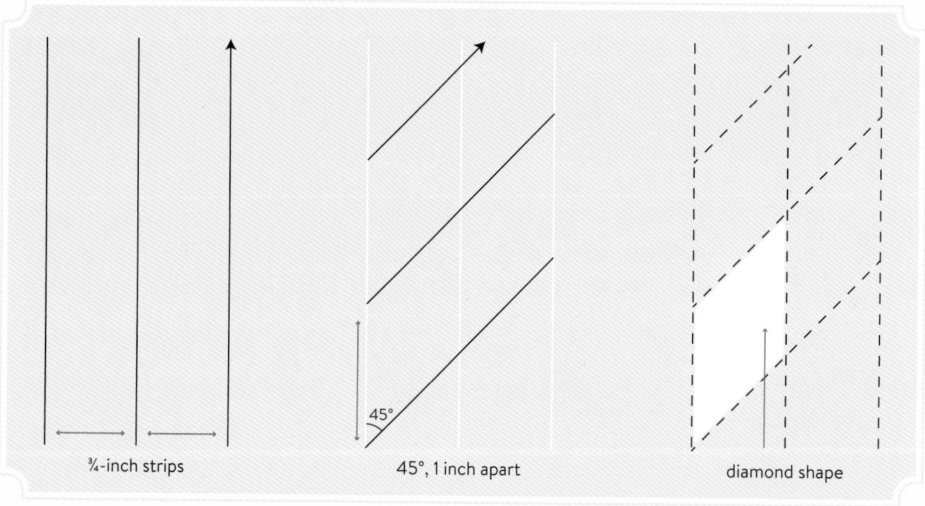

Dip the tops of the calissons in the orange blossom glaze or use a toothpick to spread the glaze over the tops. The glaze layer should be about 1⁄16 inch (1.5 millimeter) thick. Return them to the waxed or parchment paper and let them air-dry for 24 hours. Store them in an airtight container at room temperature for up to 2 weeks.

GRAPEFRUIT CONFIT

Makes about 1 cup (330 grams) in syrup,
1¾ cups (160 grams) drained

Peel of 1 small grapefruit

Pinch of salt

1 cup (200 grams) granulated sugar

½ cup (115 grams) water

¼ cup (85 grams) light corn syrup

Cut the grapefruit peels into ¼-inch (6 millimeter)-wide strips, then cut those into ¼-inch pieces. Place the peels in a small stainless-steel saucepan. Add the salt and enough cold water to cover. Bring to a boil over medium-high heat and blanch for 5 minutes once the water is boiling. Pour the mixture into a strainer and rinse in cold water. Repeat the blanching process 3 more times, without adding extra salt. The last time, leave the peels in the strainer and reserve.

Pour the sugar and water into the saucepan and bring to a boil over medium-high heat with the corn syrup and blanched grapefruit peels. Once the mixture reaches a boil, lower the heat to low and let simmer for 20 minutes. Remove the pan from the heat and cover it. Let the mixture cool overnight in the syrup. Store the cooled confit in the refrigerator for up to 3 months. Drain the peel before the adding it to recipes.

CANDIED CANTALOUPE

Makes 1½ pints (700 grams) in syrup,
about 1 pint (340 grams) drained

¾ cup (150 grams) granulated sugar

¼ cup (60 grams) water

Flesh of ½ medium-size (about 600 grams) ripe orange-fleshed cantaloupe, cut in ¼-inch (6-millimeter) pieces

Place the sugar in a medium saucepan and cover with the water. Bring the mixture to a boil, then add the diced cantaloupe. Lower the heat to low and let simmer for 10 minutes. Remove from the heat and let cool. Drain the cantaloupe well before adding to recipes. It will keep in the syrup, covered and refrigerated, for up to 1 month.

ORANGE BLOSSOM GLAZE

Makes about ½ cup (120 grams)

⅔ cup (100 grams) confectioners' sugar

1½ teaspoons (7 grams) orange blossom water

2½ teaspoons (10 grams) water

1 to 3 drops liquid, paste,
or gel food coloring (as desired)

1 teaspoon (6 grams) glycerin (see Resources, page 288)

Place all the ingredients in a bowl and stir by hand, to avoid creating a lot of bubbles, until they form a homogenous mixture. Use immediately, or cover the glaze with plastic wrap placed directly on the surface so that the glaze does not dry before time comes to dip the calissons.

Variation

ORANGE BLOSSOM CALISSONS

Add 1½ teaspoons (7 grams) of orange blossom water (see Resources, page 288) to the almond paste, and substitute ½ cup (90 grams) orange confit (see page 270) for the grapefruit confit and candied cantaloupe.

Pecan-Cinnamon Calissons

I love giving an American twist to very French treats, and can think of few recipes I've created that illustrate that more than this one. Calissons are as French as they come, and pecan and cinnamon some of the most representative flavors of the United States. These sweets make a welcome and unique addition to a holiday dessert table, and are terrific with a cup of black tea or chai.

Makes about 20 (¾-inch/2-centimeter) calissons

¾ cup (100 grams) pecan halves or pieces

¼ cup (25 grams) sliced almonds

⅔ cup (100 grams) confectioners' sugar, plus more for assembly

⅛ teaspoon (0.5 gram) fine sea salt

⅛ teaspoon (0.5 gram) ground cinnamon

1 tablespoon plus 1½ teaspoons (42 grams) apricot preserves

1 (11 x 8½-inch [28 x 22-centimeter]) sheet wafer paper (see Resources, page 288)

Frangelico Glaze (recipe follows)

Preheat the oven to 350°F (175°C).

Spread the pecans and almonds on 2 baking sheets and bake them [in the oven] until they are lightly toasted, about 5 minutes. Remove from the oven and let them cool.

Place the nuts in the bowl of a food processor and pulse about 30 times, until they are ground into a smooth paste, stopping and scraping the sides of the bowl every 5 pulses. Add the sugar, salt, cinnamon, and apricot preserves and pulse about another 30 times, until a smooth paste forms, stopping and scraping the sides of the bowl every 5 pulses, to ensure that all the ingredients are mixing smoothly. You should be able to press the dough into a ball with your hands.

Place one sheet of the wafer paper on waxed or parchment paper, shiny side up. Place half of the dough on the wafer paper, sprinkle it with confectioners' sugar, and roll it out into a rectangle about 11 x 4 inches (28 x 10 centimeters) and ⅓ inch (8.5 millimeters) thick. Repeat with the second half of the dough.

With a calisson or diamond cookie cutter (see Resources, page 288), a chef's knife, or a sharp pizza cutter, cut the dough into diamonds. If using a knife or pizza cutter, use a ruler to cut ¾-inch (2-centimeter)-wide strips parallel to each other. Then place the ruler at the bottom left of the dough on a 45-degree angle. Measure 1-inch (2.5-centimeter)-wide strips parallel to each other, and then the cut diamond shapes that form. Use the diagram on page 90 as a guide.

Dip the tops of the calissons in the Frangelico glaze or use a toothpick to spread the glaze over the tops. The glaze layer should be about 1/16 inch (1.5 millimeters) thick. Return them to the waxed or parchment paper and let them air-dry for 24 hours. Store them in an airtight container at room temperature for up to 2 weeks.

FRANGELICO GLAZE

Makes about ½ cup (125 grams)

⅔ cup (100 grams) confectioners' sugar

1 tablespoon (15 grams) Frangelico

2½ teaspoons (10 grams) water

1 to 3 drops liquid, paste,
or gel food coloring (as desired)

1 teaspoon (6 grams) glycerin
(see Resources, page 288)

Place all the ingredients in a bowl and stir by hand, to avoid creating a lot of bubbles, until they form a homogenous mixture. Use immediately, or cover the glaze with plastic wrap placed directly on the surface so that the glaze does not dry before time comes to dip the calissons.

Variation

HAZELNUT–CACAO NIB CALISSONS

Substitute ⅔ cup (90 grams) of chopped, toasted hazelnuts and ⅛ cup (20 grams) of cacao nibs for the pecans. Omit the cinnamon. Pulse the mixture about 50 times.

Raspberry Cream Macarons

Macarons

THE DELICATE AND DELICIOUS MACARON REMAINS ONE OF THE MOST POPULAR small treats over a century after its invention in France, and shows no sign of fading in appeal this side of the ocean. This chapter offers new flavor variations to our first book, *Les Petits Macarons: Colorful French Confections to Make at Home*, where you'll also find extensive information on different techniques and procedures. We are biased, but we think that if you like the macaron recipes here, you should get that book, too!

Each of the filling recipes makes enough for one batch of the base recipe.

To create the "foot" that characterizes macarons—the textured ring around the base of the shell—a nonnegligible amount of sugar is needed, which makes for sweet shells. A tangy filling offers a nice counterpoint to all that sweetness, with such acidic ingredients as raspberries, chocolate, passion fruit, or citruses. A great macaron features a perfect balance of flavors in just a couple of bites.

Follow these few tips to make your first macaron baking experience pleasant: Wait for a dry day—humidity is always challenging when baking meringue-based recipes. Use a scale to measure your ingredients. Make sure you whip your meringue thoroughly to stiff peaks. Pipe and bake just a couple of shells so that you can troubleshoot any oven or batter issues before baking the full batch (the remaining batter should be in the pastry bag so that it doesn't dry out). Ovens are widely temperamental and can cause macarons to brown. Lower the heat as needed; for every 25°F (4°C) you lessen the temperature, add 1 to 2 minutes to the baking time.

The fillings in this chapter also work very well as fillings for the tartelette doughs (pages 157–163), while the Earl Grey–Lavender Ganache tartelette filling (page 173) is fabulous in macarons.

Macaron Shells

This recipe doesn't require heating sugar, which allows even young children to help in complete safety. You can leave the shells natural, so they'll be white or speckled depending on the type of almond flour you use, or you can play with food colorings of your choosing and add those to the batter as instructed below. You'll need to use a powdered type (see Resources, page 288) for a shade darker than a pastel. My favorite way to color macarons, however, is to create a swirl effect by dropping a few drops of food coloring onto the tip of a pastry brush and striping it up the inside of the pastry bag before filling it with the batter, from the tip to about halfway up. I've managed to create stripes of five different colors, and love the joyful way in which the finished macarons resemble Italian marble. You will need four baking sheets to bake all the shells at once, but can also do with two, leaving the remaining batter in the pastry bag and tying its top closed while the first batch bakes.

Makes 40 (1¾-inch/4.5-centimeter) shells,
enough for 20 sandwiched macarons

¼ cup (77 grams) aged egg whites
(from 3 large eggs; see note)

2 teaspoons (3 grams) powdered egg whites

¼ cup plus 1 tablespoon (70 grams) granulated sugar

1⅓ loose cups (110 grams) almond flour

¾ cup medium-packed (110 grams) confectioners' sugar

1 pinch of fine sea salt

4 to 6 drops liquid, paste, or gel food coloring,
or up to ⅛ teaspoon (0.5 grams) powdered food coloring (as desired)

Line two baking sheets with silicone mats. Place each baking sheet on top of another unlined one so that they are doubled up; this insulates the macarons and evens out the oven's heat, making for a more even baking.

In the bowl of an electric mixer fitted with the whisk attachment, whisk the egg whites and powdered egg whites on medium speed until soft peaks form, about 2 minutes. Gradually add the granulated sugar and continue whisking the meringue until very stiff peaks form.

Place the almond flour, confectioners' sugar, and salt in the bowl of a food processor and pulse for 10 seconds to combine them. With a spatula, fold the dry ingredients into the meringue. If using food coloring, stop folding when the batter appears to be 90 percent incorporated, scrape the sides of the bowl, and stir in the desired coloring with 2 to 4 more strokes. The batter is ready when it is shiny (very important!) and loose enough to drop down from the spatula back to the bowl into one continuous lavalike flow. The batter should not hold any three-dimensional shape.

Spoon the batter into a piping bag fitted with a ¼ to ⅓-inch (6- to 8.5-millimeter) round tip. Fill the bag halfway, and cover the rest of the batter in the bowl while piping. Holding the tip of the bag at a 90-degree angle ¼ inch (6 millimeters) above the baking sheet, firmly squeeze it until you have a 1½-inch (4-centimeter) round about ¼ inch (6 millimeters) high. Do not move the bag while squeezing out the batter. As soon as you have reached the desired size, completely release the pressure on the bag and twist your wrist in a clockwise direction, without lifting it up. Once the batter stops flowing, stop squeezing the bag, lift, and pipe the next round, 1½ inches (4 centimeters) apart. Continue with the remaining batter. Firmly slam the baking sheets on your countertop to remove excess air and ensure that any tails settle down.

Let the macaron shells air-dry on the baking sheets for 20 minutes.

While the shells dry, preheat the oven to 350°F (175°C).

Bake for 8 minutes, then lower the heat to 275°F (135°C) and bake for 10 more minutes. Remove from the oven and let the pans cool to the touch. To easily remove the shells from the baking sheets, place them in the freezer for 15 minutes, then remove the shells with an offset spatula. If your freezer doesn't fit sheet pans, slide the silicone mat onto a cooling rack and let the shells cool completely, about 1 hour.

NOTE: To age the egg whites, separate them into a bowl or container and whisk them lightly to break them up. Cover the container in plastic wrap, poke a few holes in the plastic, and refrigerate for 3 days. To then measure them out for the recipe, place another container on a scale, zero it out, and slowly pour in the whisked aged whites until you reach the desired weight.

TO FILL AND STORE THE MACARONS

Spoon the filling into a piping bag and cut a ¼- to ½-inch (6-millimeter to 1.25-centimeter) opening in the bag, depending on the thickness and fluidity of the filling (cut it smaller for looser fillings). Such fillings as compotes and jams, which can be quite stiff, are best spooned onto the macaron shells.

Turn half of the shells flat-side up. Pipe the filling in mounds about ½ inch (1.25 centimeters) high, leaving a ¼-inch (6-millimeter) margin around the edges. Place another shell of matching size, flat-side down, onto the filling to make a sandwich. Twist lightly to sandwich the macaron together securely. Store the finished macarons in an airtight container in the refrigerator for up to 3 days, or freeze them for up to 3 weeks. Let them come to room temperature before serving.

Yuzu-Vanilla Curd Macarons

I tasted a delicious lemon-yuzu éclair at Christophe Adam's pâtisserie in Paris, and ever since have been obsessed with the tangy freshness of yuzu. I love using Pierre Hermé's technique to cool down a curd before emulsifying in the butter, which gives it a mousselike texture. You will find yuzu juice in Asian supermarkets, or if your supermarket is well stocked, in its Asian ingredient section. You can substitute passion fruit juice or purée (see Resources, page 288).

Makes about 1 cup (227 grams) filling;
enough to fill 1 batch of macarons

½ cup (100 grams) granulated sugar

½ vanilla bean

¾ cup (105 grams) yuzu juice

2 large eggs

⅓ sheet (0.7 gram) gold gelatin (see page 20)

1 cup (230 grams) ice water

½ cup (113 grams) unsalted butter,
at room temperature

1 recipe Macaron Shells
(page 101, yellow color suggested)

Place the sugar in a medium saucepan. Split the vanilla bean lengthwise and scrape out the seeds with the back of a paring knife into the sugar. Whisk in the yuzu juice and bring the mixture to a boil over medium heat.

In a heat-resistant medium bowl, whisk the eggs until combined.

Once the syrup has boiled, remove it from the heat and whisk vigorously into the eggs. Return the mixture to the saucepan and cook, whisking constantly, over medium heat until the mixture thickens and boils for 1 minute. Remove from the heat, strain it into a bowl with a fine-mesh sieve, and insert a digital or instant-read thermometer in the mixture. Let it cool until it reaches 185°F (85°C).

While the yuzu mixture cools, soften the gelatin in the ice water for 3 minutes, then strain out the excess liquid through a fine-mesh strainer. Once the yuzu is at the right temperature, stir in the gelatin. Let it cool further to 113°F (45°C), then blend in the butter with an immersion blender until it is completely incorporated and the mixture is fluffy, about 5 minutes. Cover and refrigerate for 1 day before filling the macaron shells (see page 103), which will give the curd a better texture.

Cherry–Star Anise Jam Macarons

We made a cherry-Sauternes compote at the first restaurant where I worked after pastry school, Kinkead's Restaurant in Washington, DC. I've added star anise to this version because I like its flavor with cherries. This dark red filling is particularly pretty in a macaron. To achieve the multi-colored swirl effect shown here, use the technique described on page 101.

Makes about 1 cup (227 grams) filling;
enough to fill 1 batch of macarons

¼ cup (50 grams) granulated sugar

1 teaspoon (5 grams) freshly squeezed and strained lemon juice (from ½ lemon)

2 cups (380 grams) cherries, pitted and cut into ½-inch (1.25-centimeter) pieces

1 cup (100 grams) Sauternes (or other white wine)

2 sticks cinnamon

3 star anise

1 recipe Macaron Shells (page 101, red or swirled red-purple color suggested)

Place the sugar in a medium saucepan and clip a calibrated candy thermometer to its side. Drizzle the lemon juice over the sugar and use your hands to rub it in. Add the cherries, wine, cinnamon sticks, and star anise and bring the mixture to a boil over medium heat. Stir occasionally with a heat-resistant spatula until the mixture reaches 222°F (106°C).

Remove from the heat and pour into a shallow pan to cool. Remove the cinnamon sticks and star anise before filling the macaron shells (see page 103). The filling will keep in an airtight container in the refrigerator for up to 2 weeks.

Strawberry-Rhubarb Compote Macarons

Rhubarb and strawberries are some of the first fruits to appear after winter. They are often paired both for that reason and because the sweetness of the strawberries balances the sometimes very tart rhubarb. Rhubarb is an easy-to-grow perennial—if you have a garden, try planting it. It's Anne's favorite "fruit" (it's botanically a vegetable) and she makes sure to go to her farmers' market early when it's in season, since usually only a limited quantity is available.

Makes about 1 cup (227 grams) filling;
enough to fill 1 batch of macarons

½ cup (100 grams) plus 1 tablespoon (12 grams) granulated sugar, divided

1 cup (100 grams) white wine

2 stalks (about 140 grams) rhubarb, cut into ¼-inch (6-millimeter) slices

3 sticks cinnamon

6 cloves

6 black peppercorns

½ teaspoon (2 grams) powdered pectin

½ cup (160 grams) diced strawberries (from about 8 large strawberries)

½ teaspoon (5 grams) freshly squeezed and strained lemon juice (from ½ lemon)

1 recipe Macaron Shells (page 101, pink or swirled pink-ivory-red color suggested)

Place ½ cup (100 grams) of the sugar in a medium saucepan, pour the wine around the edges of the pan, and swirl it into the center by tilting the saucepan. Add the rhubarb, cinnamon, cloves, and peppercorns and bring to a boil over medium heat. Clip a calibrated candy thermometer to the saucepan.

In a small bowl, whisk the remaining 1 tablespoon (12 grams) of sugar and the pectin until combined, then whisk the mixture into the rhubarb. Stir in the strawberries, bring back to a boil, and cook, stirring continuously, until the mixture reaches 222°F (106°C).

Remove from the heat, stir in the lemon juice, and pour into a shallow pan to cool. With a spoon, remove the spices before filling the macaron shells (see page 103). The filling will keep in an airtight container in the refrigerator for up to 1 week.

Tarte Tatin Macarons

One sleepy Sunday, I visited the town of Lamotte-Beuvron in the Loir-et-Cher in central France, where tarte Tatin was invented (a claim that every pastry shop there seemed to make). The result of this visit is this macaron filling, which evolved thanks to the way my friend Bernard Levenez (who hails from Brittany) cooks the apples in butter until they naturally caramelize from their own sweetness; he only then adds sugar to create a more complex caramel flavor.

Makes about 1 cup (227 grams) filling;
enough to fill 1 batch of macarons

2 tablespoons (28 grams) unsalted butter, divided

2 firm baking apples (such as Golden Delicious or Granny Smith), peeled, cored, and cut into ¼-inch (6-millimeter) cubes, divided

2 tablespoons (24 grams) granulated sugar, divided

1 tablespoon (15 grams) Calvados, divided

1 pinch of fleur de sel

1 recipe Macaron Shells (page 101, red or swirled red-yellow-green color suggested)

Heat a 10-inch (25-centimeter)-wide sauté pan over low heat. Add half of the butter. Once the butter has melted, add half of the apples in one layer; do not stack them. Cook until the apples begin to brown, then turn them over with a heat-resistant spatula and sprinkle half of the sugar over them. Cook until the apples caramelize lightly but are still firm. (If the apples are too crowded in the pan, they will steam rather than caramelize. To prevent this, and to allow the apples to color nicely and develop good flavor, the apples are cooked in two batches.)

Remove the pan from the heat and stir in half of the Calvados. With the spatula, gently transfer the apples to a shallow pan to cool. Wipe the sauté pan with a paper towel and repeat the process with the second half of the ingredients.

Once all of the apples are cooled, sprinkle them with the fleur de sel. Stir them to combine before filling the macaron shells (see page 103). Use right away.

Spiced Fig-Almond Cream Macarons

Flavored almond paste is one of the simplest and easiest macaron fillings to prepare; this one evolved from the dried figs rehydrated in port that I created for *Les Petits Macarons*. The combination of the creamy and buttery almond paste with the spiced fresh figs is divine.

Makes about 1 cup (227 grams) filling; enough to fill 1 batch of macarons

4 fresh, ripe figs, stemmed and cut into ½-inch (1.25-centimeter) pieces

1 packed tablespoon (12 grams) light brown sugar

¼ teaspoon (1 gram) ground cinnamon

¼ teaspoon (1.2 grams) ground nutmeg

1 large pinch of ground cloves

1 large pinch of freshly ground black pepper

¼ teaspoon (1 gram) fine sea salt

½ cup (104 grams) almond paste

2 tablespoons (28 grams) unsalted butter, at room temperature

1 recipe Macaron Shells (page 101, purple or swirled purple-brown-burgundy color suggested)

Place the figs, sugar, cinnamon, nutmeg, cloves, pepper, and salt in a medium sauté pan and let macerate for 15 minutes.

Heat the figs over medium-high heat, stirring until the sugar melts and the figs render their juices, about 5 minutes. Remove from the heat, pour the figs into a shallow pan, and let cool completely.

Once the figs are cooled, place the almond paste and butter in the bowl of an electric mixer fitted with the paddle attachment. Beat on medium speed until the mixture becomes smooth and fluffy, between 5 and 10 minutes. Add the cooled figs and mix until they are incorporated. Fill the macaron shells as directed on page 103. The filling will keep in an airtight container in the refrigerator for up to 1 week.

Raspberry Cream Macarons

I love adding basil to sweet dishes, and this recipe is no exception—it pairs extremely well with raspberries and cuts through the sweetness of the white chocolate. To showcase the flavor of the fruit in this filling, I prefer using Opalys, a low-added-sugar white chocolate made by Valrhona.

Makes about 1 cup (265 grams) filling; enough to fill 1 batch of macarons

½ cup (120 grams) raspberry purée (see Resources, page 288)

¼ packed teaspoon (1 gram) finely grated lemon zest (from ¼ lemon)

¼ teaspoon (0.3 grams) pink peppercorns, finely chopped

8 fresh basil leaves

8.8 ounces (250 grams) white chocolate, preferably Opalys, finely chopped (about 1⅔ cups chopped)

1 teaspoon (4 grams) pure vanilla extract

¼ teaspoon (1 gram) fleur de sel

½ teaspoon (7.5 grams) Framboise

1 recipe Macaron Shells (page 101, swirled pink or pink-burgundy color suggested)

Heat the raspberry purée, lemon zest, pink peppercorns, and basil in a small saucepan over medium heat and bring to a rapid boil. Let it boil for 5 minutes, then remove the basil leaves with kitchen tongs.

Remove from the heat and pour in the chocolate, vanilla, and fleur de sel. Shake the saucepan so that the chocolate is submerged. Let sit for 1 minute, then whisk rapidly from the center of the pot outward in a spiral shape until the chocolate is fully melted. Slowly drizzle and whisk in the Framboise. Pour the mixture into a shallow pan and refrigerate to let it set, about 1 hour. It should have a consistency similar to that of peanut butter, soft enough to be piped but not runny. Fill the macaron shells as direted on page 103. The filling will keep, covered and refrigerated, for up to 1 week. If you store it, bring it to room temperature 1 hour before filling the macarons.

Strawberry-Thyme Dacquoisettes

Dacquoisettes

STRAWBERRY-THYME DACQUOISETTES

PAIN D'ÉPICES DACQUOISETTES

PISTACHIO DACQUOISETTES

AS MY WELL-DOCUMENTED LOVE FOR MACARONS ATTESTS, I HAVE A FONDNESS for all things meringue and enjoy exploring techniques and flavor possibilities. It dates back to my childhood, when my maternal grandmother regularly made meringues for dessert. Dacquoise traditionally consists of ground hazelnuts folded into a meringue and baked until crispy. Praline buttercream is then spread or piped on one layer of dacquoise and topped with another, with praline and candied hazelnut adorning the whole cake. It's classic, and delicious, but a bit heavy. These dacquoisettes are smaller, lighter, and more contemporary. I also use almond or pistachio flour instead of hazelnut flour. You can use them for ice-cream sandwiches by piping them 3 inches (7.5 centimeters) wide. If you are good at piping and don't need an outline, feel free to use a silicone mat instead of parchment paper.

Strawberry-Thyme Dacquoisettes

Freeze-dried strawberries are widely available these days, but if you own a dehydrator, you can also dehydrate strawberries when they are at the height of their season and flavor and use those instead.

Makes about 35 sandwiched dacquoisettes

1 cup (180 grams) confectioners' sugar

1 cup (108 grams) almond flour

½ cup (65 grams) cornstarch

¼ teaspoon (1 gram) fine sea salt

4 large egg whites

1 tablespoon plus 2 teaspoons (8.5 grams) powdered egg whites

⅔ cup (134 grams) granulated sugar

¼ cup (18 grams) freeze-dried strawberries (see Resources, page 288), roughly chopped into ¼-inch (6-millimeter) pieces, divided

1 teaspoon (4 grams) pure vanilla extract

Leaves from 1 sprig fresh thyme or lemon thyme, roughly chopped

1 recipe Mascarpone Cream (recipe follows)

Preheat the oven to 250°F (120°C).

Trace 70 circles with a 1½-inch (4-centimeter)-wide biscuit cutter on two half-sheets of parchment paper, leaving about 1 inch (2.5 centimeters) between each circle. Flip the paper over onto two half-sheet pans.

Sift the confectioners' sugar, almond flour, cornstarch, and salt into a bowl or onto a piece of waxed paper and set aside.

In the bowl of an electric mixer fitted with the whisk attachment, whisk the egg whites and powdered egg whites on medium speed until soft peaks form, about 2 minutes. Gradually add the granulated sugar and continue whisking until a very stiff meringue forms, about 8 minutes. Add the vanilla, stop the mixer, and with a spatula fold in the dry ingredients and half of the chopped strawberries until just incorporated.

Spoon the batter into a piping bag fitted with a ½-inch (1.25-centimeter) star tip. With your piping bag ¼ inch (6 millimeters) above the sheet pan surface, quickly pipe the batter into spirals on each circle on the parchment paper, 1 inch (2.5 centimeters) apart, until the batter is used up. Sprinkle the meringues with the remaining strawberries and thyme. Immediately bake for 35 minutes, until the meringues are completely crisp. They should come off the parchment paper with no resistance and feel soft. Remove from the oven and let cool on the baking sheet. The meringues will keep in an airtight container for up to 2 days (unless your kitchen is very humid) or frozen in resealable plastic bags for up to 1 month.

ASSEMBLE THE DACQUOISETTES: Spoon the mascarpone cream in a piping bag fitted with an open ½-inch (1.25-centimeter) star tip. Pipe the cream in a spiral shape over the flat side of a baked and cooled dacquoisette. Invert a second dacquoisette, flat-side down, over the cream. Repeat with the rest of the baked dacquoisettes. Wrap them in plastic wrap and store them in the refrigerator for up to 2 days or in the freezer for up to 1 month.

MASCARPONE CREAM

Makes about ¾ cup (230 grams)

4 ounces (113 grams) white chocolate, coarsely chopped (about ¾ cup chopped)
4 ounces (113 grams) mascarpone cheese
1 teaspoon (4 grams) pure vanilla extract
⅛ teaspoon (0.5 gram) fleur de sel

Bring a pan filled halfway with water to a boil over medium-high heat. Lower the heat to low and place the chocolate in a bowl that can fit over the pan without touching the water. Let the chocolate melt halfway, paying close attention to ensure that it doesn't burn. Take the chocolate off the heat and stir until it is completely melted. Add the mascarpone, vanilla, and salt and vigorously whisk in circles until the mixture is smooth. Pour the mascarpone cream into a shallow pan so that it can set. It will keep, covered and refrigerated, for up to a week. Let it come back to room temperature for 1 hour before filling the dacquoisettes.

Pain d'Épices Dacquoisettes

Pain d'épices, or spiced bread, is often part of the *goûter*, the afternoon French snack time; a soft, golden slice gets a pat of butter and a drizzle of honey. To replicate this treat in a version that will make both kids and grown-ups happy, I pair a spiced meringue with a honey buttercream. This will make more buttercream than you need to fill the dacquoisettes, but making a one-egg-white buttercream is nearly impossible. Keep the leftover in a resealable plastic bag in the freezer for up to 2 months.

Makes about 35 sandwiched dacquoisettes

1 cup (180 grams) confectioners' sugar

1 cup (108 grams) almond flour

½ cup (65 grams) cornstarch

1 teaspoon (3 grams) ground ginger

¾ teaspoon (2 grams) Chinese 5-spice powder

⅛ teaspoon (0.5 gram) freshly ground white pepper

¼ teaspoon (1 gram) fine sea salt

4 large egg whites

1 tablespoon plus 2 teaspoons (8.5 grams) powdered egg whites

⅔ cup (134 grams) granulated sugar

1 recipe Honey Buttercream (recipe follows)

Preheat the oven to 250°F (120°C).

Trace 70 circles with a 1½-inch (4-centimeter)-wide biscuit cutter on two half-sheets of parchment paper, leaving about 1 inch (2.5 centimeters) between each circle. Flip the paper over onto two half-sheet pans.

Sift the confectioners' sugar, almond flour, cornstarch, ginger, 5-spice powder, pepper, and salt into a bowl or onto a piece of waxed paper and set aside.

In the bowl of an electric mixer fitted with the whisk attachment, whisk the egg whites and powdered egg whites on medium speed until soft peaks form, about 2 minutes. Gradually add the granulated sugar and continue whisking until a very stiff meringue forms, about 8 minutes. Stop the mixer, and with a spatula fold in the dry ingredients until just incorporated.

Spoon the batter into a piping bag fitted with a ½-inch (1.25-centimeter) star tip. With your piping bag ¼ inch (6 millimeters) above the sheet pan surface, quickly pipe the batter into spirals on each circle on the parchment paper, 1 inch (2.5 centimeters) apart, until the batter is used up. Immediately bake for 35 minutes, until the meringues are completely crisp. They should come off the parchment paper with no resistance and feel soft. Remove from the oven and let cool on the baking sheet. The meringues will keep in an airtight container for up to 2 days (unless your kitchen is very humid) or frozen in resealable plastic bags for up to 1 month.

ASSEMBLE THE DACQUOISETTES: Spoon the buttercream into a piping bag fitted with an open ½-inch (1.25-centimeter) star tip. Pipe the buttercream in a spiral shape over the flat side of a baked and cooled dacquoisette. Invert a second dacquoisette, flat-side down, over the buttercream. Repeat with the rest of the baked dacquoisettes, or with however many you desire to make at one time. Wrap them in plastic wrap and store them in the refrigerator for up to 5 days (bring them to room temperature 1 hour before serving so the buttercream can soften) or in the freezer for up to 1 month.

OPTIONAL: Crush about 10 of the cooled dacquoisettes in a food processor to create pain d'épices–flavored crumbs. Place the crumbs on a plate and roll each sandwiched dacquoisette into them; the crumbs will adhere to the buttercream, making for a lovely presentation.

HONEY BUTTERCREAM

Makes about 2 cups (630 grams)

2 large egg whites

½ cup (165 grams) honey

¾ cup (171 grams) unsalted butter, chilled, cut into 1-inch (2.5-centimeter) cubes

1 teaspoon (4 grams) pure vanilla extract

¼ teaspoon (1 gram) fine sea salt

In the bowl of an electric mixer fitted with the whisk attachment, whisk the egg whites on medium speed until soft peaks form, about 2 minutes. Lower the speed to low if the egg whites are at soft peaks before the honey is ready.

While the egg whites are whipping, heat the honey in a small saucepan over medium-high heat. Clip a calibrated candy thermometer to the pan and cook until the honey reaches 241°F (116°C), closely monitoring it.

When the honey reaches 241°F (116°C), quickly and steadily pour it down the side of the mixer bowl, with the mixer running at medium speed. Rest the lip of the saucepan on the side of the bowl so that the honey does not hit the whisk and splatter (it should run gradually down the side of the bowl). Continue whisking until stiff peaks form and the meringue is cool, about 6 minutes. Add the butter all at once, and the vanilla and salt, increase the speed to high, and whip until the mixture is fluffy and emulsified, about 12 minutes. Do not panic if it looks curdled or like it has a strange texture; keep going until the buttercream reaches the proper smooth consistency. Use right away to fill the dacquoisettes.

Pistachio Dacquoisettes

You can find pistachio flour online (see Resources, page 288), in health food stores, or make your own by grinding pistachios into a fine powder. Be careful to not grind them so much that they turn into a paste. If you want to gild the lily, roll each sandwiched dacquoisette in finely chopped pistachios or freeze-dried raspberries for a show-stopping presentation.

Makes about 35 sandwiched dacquoisettes

1 cup (180 grams) confectioners' sugar

1 cup (108 grams) pistachio flour

½ cup (65 grams) cornstarch

¼ teaspoon (1 gram) fine sea salt

4 large egg whites

1 tablespoon plus 2 teaspoons (8.5 grams) powdered egg whites

⅔ cup (134 grams) granulated sugar

½ teaspoon (2 grams) pure vanilla extract

1 recipe Raspberry Jam (recipe follows)

Preheat the oven to 250°F (120°C).

Trace 70 circles with a 1½-inch (4-centimeter)-wide biscuit cutter on two half-sheets of parchment paper, leaving about 1 inch (2.5 centimeters) between each circle. Flip the paper over onto two half-sheet pans.

Sift the confectioners' sugar, pistachio flour, cornstarch, and salt into a bowl or onto a piece of waxed paper and set aside.

In the bowl of an electric mixer fitted with the whisk attachment, whisk the egg whites and powdered egg whites on medium speed until soft peaks form, about 2 minutes. Gradually add the granulated sugar and continue whisking until a very stiff meringue forms, about 8 minutes. Add the vanilla, stop the mixer, and with a spatula fold in the dry ingredients until just incorporated.

Spoon the batter into a piping bag fitted with a ½-inch (1.25-centimeter) star tip. With your piping bag ¼ inch (6 millimeters) above the sheet pan surface, quickly pipe the batter into spirals on each circle on the parchment paper, 1 inch (2.5 centimeters) apart, until the batter is used up. Immediately bake for 35 minutes, until the meringues are completely crisp. They should come off the parchment paper with no resistance and feel soft. Remove from the oven and let cool on the baking sheet. The meringues will keep in an airtight container for up to 2 days (unless your kitchen is very humid) or frozen in resealable plastic bags for up to 1 month.

ASSEMBLE THE DACQUOISETTES: Spoon the jam into a piping bag (without a tip). Cut a ⅛-inch (3-millimeter) hole straight across the tip of the pastry bag. Pipe the jam in a spiral shape over the flat side of a baked and cooled dacquoisette. Invert a second dacquoisette, flat-side down, over the jam. Repeat with the rest of the baked dacquoisettes, or with however many you desire to make at one time. Wrap them in plastic wrap and store them in the refrigerator for up to 5 days or in the freezer for up to 1 month.

RASPBERRY JAM

Makes 1 cup (310 grams)

3 dry half-pints (510 grams) fresh raspberries or frozen and thawed raspberries

1¼ cups (250 grams) granulated sugar

1 tablespoon plus 1 teaspoon (20 grams) freshly squeezed and strained lemon juice (from ½ lemon)

Place the raspberries and sugar in a medium saucepan over medium-high heat and bring to a boil for 1 minute. Pour the mixture through a fine-mesh strainer into a bowl to strain out the raspberry seeds. Return the strained mixture to the saucepan and cook, stirring constantly with a heat-resistant spatula, for 8 to 10 minutes, until it reaches a jamlike consistency, about 217°F (103°C) on a calibrated candy thermometer, and clings to the spatula. Remove from the heat, stir in the lemon juice, and pour the jam into a shallow pan to cool. It will keep, covered and refrigerated, for up to 2 weeks.

Éclairs with Lemon Crémeux and Fresh Fruit

Éclairs, Choux, and Religieuses

PÂTE À CHOUX

BASE PASTRY CREAM

LICORICE PASTRY CREAM

PRALINE PASTRY CREAM

ROSE PASTRY CREAM

WHITE CHOCOLATE PASTRY CREAM

CASSIS CRÉMEUX

LEMON CRÉMEUX

BITTERSWEET CHOCOLATE CRÉMEUX

VANILLA FONDANT

CASSIS-CARAMEL GLAZE

SEMISWEET CHOCOLATE GLAZE

THE PILLOWY INTERIOR AND CRISP EXTERIOR OF PÂTE À CHOUX COMBINED WITH soft, rich pastry cream is as close to a perfect sweet bite as they come. Éclairs, choux (or cream puffs), and religieuses are the three best ways to enjoy such perfection. While éclairs are having a peak in popularity and have become modes of creative expression for many a pastry chef, religieuses are not as popular in this country as they are in France. This pretty and elegant dessert features a regular-size choux topped with a smaller one. A collar of fondant is said to give it its name, recalling the habit of nuns.

The recipes here allow you to mix and match fillings and glazes to create your own treats, so have some fun with your pairings. When making religieuses, which have two choux and thus can have two flavors of fillings—but one is fine, too, if you prefer—some of my favorite combinations are Licorice Pastry Cream with Bittersweet Chocolate Crémeux, Praline Pastry Cream with Lemon Crémeux, Rose Pastry Cream with Cassis Crémeux, and White Chocolate Pastry Cream with Matcha Crémeux (see page 165). All of the filling and glaze recipes make enough for one batch of the pâte à choux recipe.

PIPING AND BAKING CHOUX

Depending on your oven—some heat less strongly than others—the pâte à choux will take longer to bake, potentially adding up to 5 minutes of baking time to the recipe. The range indicated here accounts for this variation; start with the first amount of time indicated (25 or 35 minutes) and if your choux are still very soft at that point, continue baking them for up to 10 extra minutes (stay close to monitor them), until they are done.

TO PIPE 1-INCH (2.5-CENTIMETER) CHOUX: Line a baking sheet with parchment paper. Holding the pastry bag about ¾ inch (2 centimeters) above the parchment paper, pipe the dough into 1-inch (2.5-centimeter)-wide mounds spaced 1 inch apart. Bake for 35 to 40 minutes, until golden brown. A cooked choux feels light, with a firm shell, when you pick it up. Let cool completely.

TO PIPE ½-INCH (1.25-CENTIMETER) CHOUX (FOR RELIGIEUSES): Line a baking sheet with parchment paper. Holding the pastry bag about ½ inch (1.25 centimeters) above the parchment paper, pipe the dough into ½-inch-wide mounds spaced 1 inch (2.5 centimeters) apart. Bake for 25 to 30 minutes, until golden brown. A cooked choux feels light, with a firm shell, when you pick it up. Let cool completely.

TO PIPE ÉCLAIRS: Line a baking sheet with parchment paper. Holding the pastry bag at a 45-degree angle above the parchment paper, pipe the dough into a ¾-inch (2-centimeter)-wide, 2-inch (5-centimeter)-long strip. Maintain a consistent pressure on the bag as you squeeze it. When you reach 2 inches, stop the piping pressure and do not pull the bag up. Space the éclairs 1 inch (2.5 centimeters) apart. Bake for 35 to 40 minutes, until golden brown. A cooked éclair feels light, with a firm shell, when you pick it up. Let cool completely.

Pâte á Choux

The amount of eggs needed in pâte à choux varies. Not all eggs, even if all are labeled "large," have the same size yolks and whites. An egg's freshness will also impact its total yield. For this recipe, you'll need somewhere between two and three eggs, so the best thing to do is to whisk three eggs together and pour that mixture into the dough a little at a time, rather than risk cracking whole eggs directly into it and having too much with a whole third one. When you've reached the right texture, your pâte à choux should rise to a perfect puff in the oven.

Makes about 30 choux, 30 éclairs, or 18 religieuses

¾ cup plus 1 tablespoon (185 grams) milk

6 tablespoons (84 grams) unsalted butter

½ teaspoon (2 grams) fine sea salt

3 large eggs

¾ cup plus 1 tablespoon (115 grams) all-purpose flour

1 scant tablespoon (10 grams) granulated sugar

Preheat the oven to 375°F (190°C).

Combine the milk, butter, and salt in a large saucepan over medium heat and bring to a boil. While the mixture is heating, whisk the eggs in a bowl. Once the milk boils, remove the pot from the heat and immediately add the flour and sugar all at once, stirring with a wooden spoon until a smooth ball forms.

Transfer the dough to the bowl of an electric mixer fitted with the paddle attachment. With the mixer running at medium speed, pour in two thirds of the eggs and mix until smooth. Draw a spatula through the dough; it should flow without leaving a shape in the dough. If it doesn't, pour in a little more of the eggs, mix, and test again.

Spoon the batter into a piping bag fitted with a ½-inch (1.25-centimeter) round tip (alternatively, cut a ½-inch opening in the bag). Pipe and bake as directed on page 135.

PIPING TIP

Pâte à choux is sticky, so it helps to "glue" your parchment paper to the baking sheet by piping a small amount of the dough under the paper in each corner. That way it will not lift every time you pipe a choux or éclair.

TO FILL THE CHOUX OR ÉCLAIRS: Spoon the pastry cream or crémeux into a piping bag fitted with a ¼-inch (6-millimeter) round or star tip. Make a small hole at the bottom of a choux or cut a slit on the bottom or side of an éclair with a paring knife, and pipe in the filling until full.

TO GLAZE THE CHOUX OR ÉCLAIRS: Place the fondant or glaze in a bowl, following the directions of each recipe to make sure that it has the right consistency. Hold a choux or éclair with one hand and dip it, top-side down, into the fondant or glaze. Let the excess drip off, dip again if needed, and then place the choux or éclair, top-side up, on a baking sheet or wire rack to set. If you've never done it before, the first ones you glaze might not be as beautiful as those you see in shops or online, but you'll quickly get the hang of it.

TO ASSEMBLE THE RELIGIEUSES: Fill an equal amount of large and small choux, then glaze the small choux. Spoon or pipe a dollop of glaze on top of the largest choux, and place the small ones on top.

Base Pastry Cream

This vanilla pastry cream is wonderful on its own or with the flavoring ideas that follow to fill your choux or éclairs. Enjoy any leftover pastry cream with berries or on a slice of tea cake. It's important to cook the cornstarch completely, or the finished cream will feel grainy to the tongue or won't set up properly; make sure to let it come to a boil for a full minute.

Makes about 1½ cups (340 grams)

1 large egg

3 large egg yolks

¼ cups (29 grams) cornstarch

¼ teaspoon (1 gram) fine sea salt

1⅓ cups (308 grams) milk

⅓ cup (74 grams) granulated sugar

2 tablespoons (28 grams) unsalted butter

½ teaspoon (2 grams) pure vanilla extract

Fit an electric mixer with the paddle attachment.

Place the egg and egg yolks in a medium bowl and whisk in the cornstarch and salt.

Whisk together the milk and sugar in a medium saucepan over medium heat and bring to a boil. Remove from the heat and immediately whisk the hot milk into the egg mixture, doing so vigorously to avoid lumps. Return the mixture to the pan and bring to a boil over medium heat, whisking constantly. The bubbles will subside; the mixture will thicken, then begin to boil. Let it boil for 1 minute, whisking vigorously.

Remove from the heat and transfer to the bowl of the prepared electric mixer. Beat in the butter and vanilla on medium speed, continuing to mix until the pastry cream has cooled. If not using right away, place a piece of plastic wrap directly on the surface of the cream to prevent a skin from forming, and refrigerate for up to 4 days.

Variation

PRALINE PASTRY CREAM

Beat in ⅓ cup (80 grams) praline paste (recipe follows, or store-bought) when you add the butter and vanilla. Makes 1¾ cups (420 grams).

PRALINE PASTE

Praline paste consists of toasted hazelnuts stirred into a caramel that is then ground when cool. It is sweet, complex, and nutty. If you choose to not make our own for this recipe, store-bought (see Resources, page 288) will work just fine. You'll end up with more than you need for the Praline Pastry Cream (see above), and the extra praline paste tastes great on buttered toast dipped in hot chocolate.

Makes 1¾ cups (397 grams)

1 cup (140 grams) blanched hazelnuts, toasted (see page 20)

1 cup (200 grams) granulated sugar

¼ cup (58 grams) water

Line a baking sheet with a silicone baking mat or parchment paper.

In a food processor, grind the hazelnuts until fine.

Place the sugar in a small saucepan, pour the water around the edges of the pan, and swirl it into the center by tilting the pot to dissolve the sugar. Bring the syrup to a boil over medium heat. Clip a calibrated candy thermometer to the pan and cook until the sugar reaches 335°F (168°C). Immediately remove from the heat and stir in the ground hazelnuts. Pour the mixture onto the prepared baking sheet and let cool for about 25 minutes.

In a food processor, finely grind the cooled praline, continuously pulsing on and off and stopping to scrape the bowl every 5 pulses. The mixture will gradually come together into a smooth paste in 15 to 25 minutes, depending on the power of your processor and the newness of the blade. Once ready, transfer it to a resealable container and keep refrigerated for up to 2 months.

Variation

LICORICE PASTRY CREAM

With a chef's knife, roughly chop 2 tablespoons (10 grams) of shredded licorice root into ½-inch (1.25-centimeter) pieces. Increase the milk to 1½ cups (230 grams). Bring the milk and licorice to a boil, then turn off the heat and let steep for 30 minutes. Blend the mixture (using either a standard or immersion blender) completely, then strain it into a bowl through a fine-mesh sieve or a chinois. Whisk in the sugar and proceed with the recipe. Makes 1½ cups (230 grams).

Variation

ROSE PASTRY CREAM

Add 1 teaspoon (0.5 gram) of rose water when you beat in the butter and vanilla. Optional: Stir in 1 teaspoon (0.5 gram) of chopped organic rose petals when the pastry cream is cool. Makes 1½ cups (230 grams).

Variation

WHITE CHOCOLATE PASTRY CREAM

Finely chop 5.3 ounces (150 grams) of white chocolate and place in the bowl of the electric mixer with the butter and vanilla. Omit the granulated sugar. When the pastry cream is cooked, pour it over the chocolate and let sit for 1 minute, then turn on the mixer to melt the chocolate and butter. Let the mixer run until the pastry cream is cool. Makes 1¾ cups (380 grams).

To Make Ahead

Freeze the piped raw choux or éclairs while on the baking sheet. Once frozen, transfer them to a resealable freezer-safe plastic bag and keep for up to 2 months. They do not need to thaw before baking. Proceed with the baking instructions.

Unfilled baked choux or éclairs can be frozen in a resealable freezer-safe plastic bag for up to 2 months. Reheat them by placing them in a 350°F (175°C) oven for about 8 minutes, until they are crisped on the outside.

Once filled, eat choux or éclairs within a day or they will go soggy.

Bittersweet Chocolate Crémeux

A crémeux is a chocolate- and gelatin-based filling that is velvety smooth, almost like a pudding. I love its texture and how it carries flavor, so use it in many applications. My favorite chocolate for this recipe is Valrhona Araguani 72 percent, from Venezuela. Chop it in a food processor so that it is very fine.

Makes 1¼ cups (284 grams)

1 sheet (2 grams) gold gelatin (see page 20)

2 cups (460 grams) ice water

2.5 ounces (70 grams) bittersweet chocolate, finely chopped (about ½ cup chopped)

4 large egg yolks

⅓ cup (80 grams) heavy whipping cream

½ cup (115 grams) milk

Soften the gelatin in the ice water for 3 minutes. Strain out the excess liquid with a fine-mesh strainer. Put the hydrated gelatin and the chocolate in a medium bowl.

In a heat-resistant medium bowl, whisk the egg yolks until combined. Heat the cream and milk in a small saucepan over medium heat and bring to a boil. Remove the mixture from the heat and whisk it little by little into the eggs, going slowly to temper the eggs and not cook them. Return the mixture to the saucepan and cook, stirring constantly with a wooden spoon, until it reaches 180°F (82°C) on a digital or instant-read thermometer. With a fine-mesh sieve, strain the mixture into the chocolate. Let sit for 1 minute, then whisk from the center to the edges of the bowl, until the crémeux is smooth and homogenous. Pour it in a shallow pan to cool, pressing a piece of plastic wrap onto its surface so that a skin doesn't form. Once cool enough, place the pan in the refrigerator and let the crémeux set for 2 hours before filling the choux.

Cassis Crémeux

If you have any of this crémeux left over after filling, you should not be afraid to eat it with a spoon, or with berries.

Makes about 1½ cups (340 grams)

1 sheet (2 grams) gold gelatin (see page 20)

1 cup (230 grams) ice water

3.5 ounces (100 grams) white chocolate, finely chopped (about ⅔ cup chopped)

4 large egg yolks

⅛ cup (25 grams) granulated sugar

½ cup (120 grams) heavy whipping cream

¼ cup (60 grams) cassis purée (see Resources, page 288)

Follow the Bittersweet Chocolate Crémeux procedure (page 148).

Variation

LEMON CRÉMEUX

Substitute ⅓ cup (80 grams) of freshly squeezed and strained lemon juice for the cassis purée, and add 1 teaspoon (4 grams) of pure vanilla extract with the white chocolate and gelatin. Makes about 1½ cups (340 grams). (Pictured on page 132 with éclairs and fresh fruit.)

Vanilla Fondant

Fondant is thicker than a ganache and is frequently used to top éclairs, because it will not drip on their sides. You can color it however you please, which makes it very versatile when you want to serve choux or éclairs at a party; it can take on any seasonal (think Easter or Halloween) or thematic (a wedding's colors at a bridal shower, for example) hue. This recipe is inspired by the wonderful one in Peter Greweling's *Chocolates and Confections.* Wrap any excess in plastic wrap and store in a tight container for up to 2 months at room temperature.

Makes about 1¾ cups (540 grams)

2½ cups (500 grams) granulated sugar

½ vanilla bean

⅔ cup (150 grams) water

½ cup (85 grams) light corn syrup

½ teaspoon (2 grams) fine sea salt

4 to 6 drops liquid, paste,
or gel food coloring (as desired)

1 to 2 tablespoons (12 to 24 grams) water

Place the sugar in a medium saucepan. Split the vanilla bean lengthwise and scrape out the seeds with the back of a paring knife into the sugar. Slowly and carefully pour the water in a spiral motion from the edges of the pan to its center, without moving the pan. Add the corn syrup and salt. Clip a calibrated candy thermometer to the pan and cook over medium heat until the mixture reaches 237°F (114°C).

Pour the cooked mixture into the bowl of an electric mixer, insert the thermometer into the fondant, and let cool at room temperature until it reaches 120°F (49°C). Do not stir. Fit the mixer with the paddle attachment and beat on low speed until the mixture turns into an opaque paste, about 15 minutes. It will thicken and start to fall apart. If not using right away, wrap tightly in plastic wrap and freeze for up to 2 months.

Place the fondant in the bowl of a food processor with the food coloring and process it until smooth. Check a bit with a spoon—the fondant should have the fluidity of a ganache and be opaque. It should coat the back of the spoon to the point that you no longer see the wood or metal. If necessary, add a few drops of water at a time to thin it out. The exact amount of water will depend on how warm the mixture gets in the food processor, which varies based on the size of the bowl. If you add too much water, you risk overthinning the fondant, which may cause drips as you dip. When the fondant is correctly thinned out, the top of any choux dipped in it should be opaque, not translucent, and hold a horizontal line without drips. When ready, you can pour the fondant in a bowl before dipping, but it's easy enough to do so from the bowl of the processor as well.

Cassis-Caramel Glaze

The cassis in this glaze gives it a beautiful purple color. It will be well worth it to source out cassis purée. The glaze also nicely varies from a chocolate glaze or vanilla fondant and will elevate even the simplest vanilla pastry cream.

Makes about 1 cup (227 grams)

1 sheet (2 grams) gold gelatin (see page 20)

1 cup (230 grams) ice water

3 tablespoons (45 grams) cassis purée (see Resources, page 288)

2 tablespoons (30 grams) heavy whipping cream

½ cup (100 grams) granulated sugar

3 tablespoons (36 grams) water

Soften the gelatin in the ice water for 3 minutes, then strain out the excess liquid through a fine-mesh strainer.

In a medium saucepan, bring the cassis purée and cream to a boil over medium heat. Set aside when it boils. The cream needs to be warm when the caramel is ready, so do not do this too far ahead.

Place the sugar in a medium saucepan, pour the water around the edges of the pan, and swirl it into the center by tilting the pot. Clip a calibrated candy thermometer to the pan and cook over medium heat until the sugar reaches the caramel stage, about 340°F (171°C). When ready, immediately stop the cooking process by pouring the caramel over the warm cassis mixture. Stir thoroughly to ensure that the caramel is completely melted, placing the saucepan over low heat if necessary.

Remove from the heat and stir in the hydrated gelatin until it is melted. Pour the glaze in a shallow pan to cool. It's best to use right away, but it will keep, covered and refrigerated, for up to 1 week.

Semisweet Chocolate Glaze

This shiny, versatile glaze freezes and thaws well. It needs to be refrigerated overnight before using, so plan ahead. If you have any extra after glazing the choux or éclairs, use it over ice cream.

Makes about 1¼ cups (300 grams)

3 sheets (6 grams) gold gelatin (see page 20)

2 cups (460 grams) ice water

1.8 ounces (50 grams) semisweet chocolate, finely chopped (about ⅓ cup chopped)

⅔ cup (130 grams) granulated sugar

½ cup (120 grams) heavy whipping cream

Edible gold leaves (optional)

Black edible glitter (optional)

Soften the gelatin in the ice water for 3 minutes, then strain out the excess liquid through a fine-mesh strainer. Place the hydrated gelatin and the chocolate in a medium heatproof bowl.

Place the sugar in a medium saucepan, pour the cream around the edges of the pan, and swirl it into the center by tilting the pot. Stir carefully to dissolve the sugar, clean the sides of the pan with a pastry brush dipped in water, and clip on a calibrated candy thermometer. Cook over medium heat until the mixture reaches 219°F (104°C).

Pour the hot sugar mixture over the chocolate, let sit for 1 minute, then blend with an immersion blender until smooth. Let cool completely at room temperature, then cover and refrigerate at least overnight or up to 1 week. It will also keep in the freezer for up to 2 months. To use, reheat to 50°F (10°C) over a double boiler (see page 18).

After glazing the choux or éclairs, decorate with a gold leaf or with glitter, if desired.

Pineapple-Apple-Cardamom Tortes

TARTELETTES AND TORTES

VANILLA SWEET DOUGH

COCOA SWEET DOUGH

COCONUT SWEET DOUGH

CORNMEAL SWEET DOUGH

CITRUS-PISTACHIO SWEET DOUGH

STRAWBERRY-MATCHA TARTELETTES

BLOOD ORANGE–MERINGUE TARTELETTES

WHITE CHOCOLATE–GRAPEFRUIT
CRÉMEUX TARTELETTES

EARL GREY TEA–LAVENDER GANACHE TARTELETTES

GRAND MARNIER–MAPLE-NUT TORTES

PINEAPPLE-APPLE-CARDAMOM TORTES

APRICOT-THYME TORTES

SAFFRON-RAISIN-CARAMEL TORTES

TARTELETTES ARE OPEN FACED, WHEREAS TORTES ARE COVERED WITH A LAYER OF dough. Tortes are like mini pies and can be served still warm; they are more rustic and homey. The open-face tartelettes are more sophisticated and perfect for company; you can decorate them with a touch of gold leaf or piped decorations. Mix and match them on a tray for a perfect tea service. A sweet dough (*pâte sucrée*) is the perfect foil to a wide range of fillings, from custards to nuts to fruits; it is one of the most basic recipes of the pastry kitchen. To add some variety, and because I am sure you already have a favorite tart dough, I developed flavored versions: vanilla, cocoa, coconut, cornmeal, and citrus-pistachio. The flavor combinations offered by pairing one of those with one of the fillings are endless; you should feel free to experiment based on your own preferences. If you want a place to start, try the coconut dough with pineapple and the chocolate dough with the Earl Grey–lavender ganache. My own favorite dough is the slightly crunchy cornmeal one, which I first encountered in a cookie form while training at Le Bernardin in New York. It pairs well with all the fruit fillings—apricot being my favorite.

I typically make tartelettes in small barquette molds (about 2¾ inches/ 7 centimeters long), but you can also use round, square, or any other shape of tartelette molds you have or want to buy. As long as the molds are between 1½ and 3 inches (4 and 7.5 centimeters), play with any shape you'd like. You will get slightly more or fewer tartelettes depending on the yield of the dough, but the difference is minimal. You can always reroll the dough and rechill it if needed, to roll out more. A mini-muffin pan will work well for both tartelettes and tortes.

Vanilla Sweet Dough

This dough goes with anything—I think of it like vanilla ice cream, which goes with every dessert. Try it with Strawberry-Matcha (page 165) and White Chocolate–Grapefruit Crémeux (page 171) fillings.

Makes about 30 (1½-inch/4-centimeter) tartelettes
or 18 (2-inch/5-centimeter) tortes

4 tablespoons (56 grams) unsalted butter, at room temperature

¼ cup (45 grams) confectioners' sugar

½ vanilla bean

1 large egg, whisked

1 cup plus 1 tablespoon (145 grams) all-purpose flour

⅛ teaspoon (0.5 gram) fine sea salt

⅛ teaspoon (0.5 gram) baking powder

Place the butter and sugar in the bowl of an electric mixer. Split the vanilla bean lengthwise and scrape out the seeds with the back of a paring knife into the sugar. Fit the mixer with the paddle attachment and cream the butter and sugar on medium speed until the mixture becomes pale and fluffy, 5 to 10 minutes. Lower the speed to low and gradually incorporate the egg, then increase the speed back to medium and beat until the mixture is again fluffy.

In a medium bowl, stir together the flour, salt, and baking powder. Turn off the mixer, add the dry ingredients, and then mix on low speed until everything is just combined, about 30 seconds. Remove the dough from the mixer, pat it into a flat ½-inch (1.25-centimeter)-thick disk, wrap it in plastic wrap, and refrigerate for 30 minutes to chill the dough and relax the gluten it contains and rechill the butter.

Cut the dough into quarters so that you can work with small amounts at a time, and keep the rest chilled. Wrapped tightly in plastic wrap, it will keep in the freezer for up to 2 months.

TO MAKE CHOCOLATE CURLS

Chocolate curls are an easy yet impressive way to decorate filled tartelettes. Buy a block of couverture chocolate. Rub your clean hand onto the side of the block to warm it up until it is shiny, then use a vegetable peeler in a downward sweeping motion to create curls. Store them in an airtight container at room temperature keeping them away from sources of heat.

Cocoa Sweet Dough

This chocolate dough is perfect for the Blood Orange–Meringue (page 168) filling and the Earl Grey Tea–Lavender Ganache (page 173).

Makes about 30 (1½-inch/4-centimeter) tartelettes
or 18 (2-inch/5-centimeter) tortes

4 tablespoons (56 grams) unsalted butter, at room temperature

¼ cup (45 grams) confectioners' sugar

1 large egg, whisked

¾ cup plus 2 tablespoons (121 grams) all-purpose flour

⅛ cup (14 grams) unsweetened cocoa powder

¼ teaspoon (1 gram) fine sea salt

⅛ teaspoon (0.5 gram) baking powder

In the bowl of an electric mixer fitted with the paddle attachment, cream the butter and sugar on medium speed until the mixture becomes pale and fluffy, 5 to 10 minutes. Lower the speed to low and gradually incorporate the egg, then increase the speed back to medium and beat until the mixture is again fluffy.

In a medium bowl, stir together the flour, cocoa powder, salt, and baking powder. Turn off the mixer, add the dry ingredients, and then mix on low speed until everything is just combined, about 30 seconds. Remove the dough from the mixer, pat it into a flat ½-inch (1.25-centimeter)-thick disk, wrap it in plastic wrap, and refrigerate for 30 minutes to chill the dough and relax the gluten it contains and rechill the butter.

Cut the dough into quarters so that you can work with small amounts at a time, and keep the rest chilled. Wrapped tightly in plastic wrap, it will keep in the freezer for up to 2 months.

Coconut Sweet Dough

Try this dough in Pineapple-Apple-Cardamom Tortes (page 178) for a complete island-like flavor experience.

Makes about 30 (1½-inch/4-centimeter) tartelettes
or 18 (2-inch/5-centimeter) tortes

4 tablespoons (56 grams) unsalted butter, at room temperature

¼ cup (45 grams) confectioners' sugar

1 large egg, whisked

1 cup (135 grams) all-purpose flour

½ cup (38 grams) unsweetened shredded coconut

¼ teaspoon (1 gram) fine sea salt

⅛ teaspoon (0.5 gram) baking powder

In the bowl of an electric mixer fitted with the paddle attachment, cream the butter and sugar on medium speed until the mixture becomes pale and fluffy, 5 to 10 minutes. Lower the speed to low and gradually incorporate the egg, then increase the speed back to medium and beat until the mixture is again fluffy.

In a medium bowl, stir together the flour, coconut, salt, and baking powder. Turn off the mixer, add the dry ingredients, and then mix on low speed until everything is just combined, about 30 seconds. Remove the dough from the mixer, pat it into a flat ½-inch (1.25-centimeter)-thick disk, wrap it in plastic wrap, and refrigerate for 30 minutes to chill the dough and relax the gluten it contains and rechill the butter.

Cut the dough into quarters so that you can work with small amounts at a time, and keep the rest chilled. Wrapped tightly in plastic wrap, it will keep in the freezer for up to 2 months.

Cornmeal Sweet Dough

This dough has a bit of texture, thanks to the cornmeal. Try it in Apricot-Thyme Tortes (page 181) or with a Blood Orange–Meringue filling (page 168).

Makes about 30 (1½-inch/4-centimeter) tartelettes
or 18 (2-inch/5-centimeter) tortes

4 tablespoons (56 grams) unsalted butter, at room temperature
¼ cup (45 grams) confectioners' sugar
1 large egg, whisked
2 tablespoons (30 grams) heavy whipping cream
¾ cup (102 grams) all-purpose flour
⅓ cup (60 grams) yellow cornmeal
⅛ teaspoon (1 gram) fine sea salt

In the bowl of an electric mixer fitted with the paddle attachment, cream the butter and sugar on medium speed until the mixture becomes pale and fluffy, 5 to 10 minutes). Lower the speed to low and gradually incorporate the egg and cream, then increase the speed back to medium and beat until the mixture is again fluffy.

In a medium bowl, stir together the flour, cornmeal, and salt. Turn off the mixer, add the dry ingredients, and then mix on low speed until everything is just combined, about 30 seconds. Remove the dough from the mixer, pat it into a flat ½-inch (1.25-centimeter)-thick disk, wrap it in plastic wrap, and refrigerate for 30 minutes to chill the dough and relax the gluten it contains and rechill the butter.

Cut the dough into quarters so that you can work with small amounts at a time, and keep the rest chilled. Wrapped tightly in plastic wrap, it will keep in the freezer for up to 2 months.

Citrus-Pistachio Sweet Dough

You can use any nut you'd like in this recipe, with or without citrus zest. Try it with lime zest and macadamia nuts, orange zest and hazelnuts, or walnuts on their own.

Makes about 30 (1½-inch/4-centimeter) tartelettes or 18 (2-inch/5-centimeter) tortes

4 tablespoons (56 grams) unsalted butter, at room temperature

¼ cup (45 grams) confectioners' sugar

2 packed teaspoons (8 grams) finely grated orange zest (from 1 orange)

1 packed teaspoon (4 grams) finely grated lemon zest (from 1 lemon)

1 large egg, whisked

¾ cup plus 1 tablespoon (111 grams) all-purpose flour

⅓ cup (50 grams) pistachio flour

⅛ teaspoon (1 gram) fine sea salt

⅛ teaspoon (0.5 gram) baking powder

In the bowl of an electric mixer fitted with the paddle attachment, cream the butter, sugar, and orange and lemon zests on medium speed until the mixture becomes pale and fluffy, 5 to 10 minutes. Lower the speed to low and gradually incorporate the egg, then increase the speed back to medium and beat until the mixture is again fluffy.

In a medium bowl, stir together the all-purpose flour, pistachio flour, salt, and baking powder. Turn off the mixer, add the dry ingredients, and then mix on low speed until everything is just combined, about 30 seconds. Remove the dough from the mixer, pat it into a flat ½-inch (1.25-centimeter)-thick disk, wrap it in plastic wrap, and refrigerate for 30 minutes to relax the gluten it contains and rechill the butter.

Cut the dough into quarters so that you can work with small amounts at a time, and keep the rest chilled. Wrapped tightly in plastic wrap, it will keep in the freezer for up to 2 months.

BAKING TARTELETTES

Preheat the oven to 350°F (175°C). Arrange 2-inch (5-centimeter) tartelette or barquette pans in front of you. You will have enough dough to make about 48 tartelettes, if you rechill and reroll the dough after the first rolling.

Place one sheet of parchment on your work surface and lightly flour it. Place the dough on top of it, then lightly flour the dough. Place a second piece of parchment on top, then roll the dough out until it is about 1⁄16 inch (1.5 millimeter) thick. If the dough sticks to the paper and doesn't roll out, flour it again on both sides. Refrigerate for 10 to 15 minutes to rechill the dough, then peel off both sheets of paper.

Working quickly, cut the dough into rectangles that are about 3 inches long and 1½ inches wide (7.5 by 4 centimeters) (or in any shape to match your tartelette pans, about ¾ inch/2 centimeters larger than the size of the pan). Place each piece in a tartelette pan. Lightly flour your fingertips and press the dough into the pans. Be careful to not leave air pockets between the dough and the pan. Freeze the tartelettes for 15 minutes before baking. Or, at this point, you can wrap the dough-lined molds tightly with plastic wrap and freeze them for up to 1 month.

Bake for 10 to 11 minutes, until golden brown. Remove from the oven and let cool for 5 minutes. If using metals pans, tap the edges of the pans on the table to carefully unmold the tartelettes. If using silicone molds, carefully peel them off. Store the baked, unfilled tartelettes in an airtight container at room temperature for 2 to 3 days. Once filled, eat within a few hours or they'll get too soft.

ROLLING OUT TORTES

Place one sheet of parchment paper on your work surface and lightly flour it. Place the dough on top of it, then lightly flour the top of the dough. Place a second piece of parchment on top, then roll the dough out until it is about 1⁄16 inch (1.5 millimeters) thick. If the dough sticks to the paper and doesn't roll out, flour it again on both sides. Refrigerate for 10 to 15 minutes to rechill the dough, then peel off both sheets of paper. Proceed with the recipe.

Strawberry-Matcha Tartelettes

Strawberry and matcha (green tea powder) are a combination frequently seen in France and in French bakeries in Japan—undoubtedly a crossover of influences. Matcha can taste bitter to some palates, so sweet strawberries help balance that quality and make the flavor more universally loved.

Makes about 30
(1½-inch/4-centimeter) tartelettes

WHITE CHOCOLATE–MATCHA CRÉMEUX FILLING

1 sheet (2 grams) gold gelatin (see page 20)

2 cups (460 grams) ice water

3.5 ounces (100 grams) white chocolate, finely chopped (about ⅔ cup chopped)

4 large egg yolks

⅓ cup (77 grams) milk

⅓ cup (80 grams) heavy whipping cream

2 teaspoons (4 grams) matcha powder

1 recipe Vanilla Sweet Dough (page 157), prebaked in tartelette shells

GARNISH

4 ripe strawberries

1 tablespoon (25 grams) apricot preserves

1 tablespoon (12 grams) water

TO MAKE THE FILLING: Soften the gelatin in the ice water for 3 minutes, then strain out the excess liquid through a fine-mesh strainer. Place the hydrated gelatin and chocolate in a medium bowl.

In a heat-resistant medium bowl, whisk the egg yolks until combined. Heat the milk and cream in a small saucepan over medium heat. Whisk in the matcha powder and bring to a boil. Remove the mixture from the heat and whisk it little by little into the eggs, going slowly to temper the eggs and not cook them. Return the mixture to the saucepan and cook, stirring constantly with a wooden spoon, until it reaches 180°F (82°C) on a digital or instant-read thermometer. With a fine-mesh sieve, strain the mixture into the chocolate. Let sit for 1 minute, then whisk from the center to the edges of the bowl, until the crémeux is smooth and homogenous. Pour it in a shallow pan to cool. Once cool enough, place the pan in the refrigerator and let the crémeux set for 2 hours.

Spoon the crémeux into a piping bag fitted with a ½-inch (1.25-centimeter) round tip (alternatively, cut a ½-inch opening in the bag) and pipe it into the tartelette shells.

TO GARNISH: Gently rinse the strawberries in cold water and pat them dry on a kitchen towel. Hull them with a paring knife and slice evenly into ⅛-inch (3-millimeter)-thick slices, keeping the slices together. Gently press down on the slices with your finger to slightly fan them out, then lift a few slices with the tip of your knife and arrange them over the matcha crémeux. Repeat until all the tartelettes are done.

Heat the apricot preserves and water in a small saucepan or in the microwave until the mixture is fluid. Dip a pastry brush into the preserves, let the excess drip back into the pot, and lightly glaze the top of the strawberries.

Blood Orange–Meringue Tartelettes

This is my twist on Key lime pie. Blood oranges are available only during a short season every winter, so when you find them, grate their zest and squeeze their juice, then freeze the zest in plastic bags and the juice in ice cube trays. Strain the juice so that the pulp doesn't affect the texture of the curd. You can substitute any citrus juice, as well as passion fruit juice, in the same proportion.

Makes about 30
(1½-inch/4-centimeter) tartelettes

2.7 ounces (75 grams) white chocolate, finely chopped (about ½ cup chopped)

Juice of 1 blood orange (60 grams), strained

Finely grated zest of 1 blood orange (4 grams)

2 large egg yolks

1 tablespoon (14 grams) unsalted butter

1 recipe Citrus-Pistachio Sweet Dough (page 162), prebaked in tartelette shells

Brown Sugar Italian Meringue (recipe follows)

Place the chocolate in a medium bowl.

Whisk together the blood orange juice, blood orange zest, and egg yolks in a medium stainless-steel saucepan until they are homogenized and smooth. Set over medium heat, whisking constantly, and cook until the mixture comes to a boil, about 8 minutes. Once it boils, whisk it vigorously for 1 minute over the heat. Remove from the heat, stir in the butter, and with a fine-mesh sieve, strain the mixture into the chocolate. Let sit for 1 minute, then whisk from the center to the edges of the bowl, until the curd is smooth and homogenous. Pour it in a shallow pan to cool. Let it cool completely at room temperature.

Spoon the filling into a piping bag without a tip. Cut a ⅛-inch (3-millimeter) hole straight across the tip of the pastry bag. Pipe the curd into the tartelette shells and top with Brown Sugar Italian Meringue.

BROWN SUGAR ITALIAN MERINGUE

You will have some extra, but it is very difficult to make a meringue with only one egg white. You can use it to ice cupcakes or make a baked Alaska, or pipe it on a parchment paper–lined baking sheet and bake at 250°F (120°C) for 45 minutes to make meringues that will keep in an airtight container well protected from humidity for about four days.

Makes about 1 cup (227 grams)

2 large egg whites

½ packed cup (110 grams) light brown sugar

¼ cup (50 grams) water

1 teaspoon (4 grams) pure vanilla extract

1 pinch of fine sea salt

In the bowl of an electric mixer fitted with the whisk attachment, whisk the egg whites on medium speed until soft peaks form, about 2 minutes. Lower the speed to low if the egg whites are at soft peaks before the sugar is ready.

While the egg whites are whipping, place the sugar in a small saucepan, pour the water around the edges of the pan toward the center in a spiral motion. Heat over medium-high heat. Clip a calibrated candy thermometer to the pan and cook until the sugar reaches 241°F (116°C), closely monitoring it.

When the sugar reaches 241°F (116°C), quickly and steadily pour it down the side of the mixer bowl, with the mixer running at medium speed. Rest the lip of the saucepan on the side of the bowl so that the sugar does not hit the whisk and splatter (it should run gradually down the side of the bowl). Continue whisking until stiff peaks form and the meringue is cool and thick, about 15 minutes. Add the vanilla and salt and spoon the mixture into a piping bag fitted with a rose tip. Pipe the meringue as desired to decorate the tartelettes. If desired, lightly torch the top of the meringue with a small handheld torch, of the variety sold in crème brûlée kit, for example.

White Chocolate–Grapefruit Crémeux Tartelettes

Think of a crémeux as a hybrid between crème anglaise and ganache—it contains chocolate, eggs, and gelatin. The combination gives it fudginess, without the gelatin overwhelming the texture. It's easy to make in a variety of flavors and freezes well.

Makes about 30
(1½-inch/4-centimeter) tartelettes

1 sheet (2 grams) gold gelatin (see page 20)

2 cups (460 grams) ice water

3.5 ounces (100 grams) white chocolate, finely chopped (about ⅔ cup chopped)

4 large egg yolks

½ cup (120 grams) heavy whipping cream

¼ cup (60 grams) freshly squeezed and strained grapefruit juice (from ½ grapefruit)

Finely grated zest of ½ grapefruit (3 grams)

1 recipe Cocoa Sweet Dough (page 159), prebaked in tartelette shells

Chocolate curls (optional, page 158)

Soften the gelatin in the ice water for 3 minutes, then strain out the excess liquid with a fine-mesh strainer. Place the hydrated gelatin and chocolate in a medium bowl.

In a heat-resistant medium bowl, whisk the egg yolks until combined. Heat the cream, grapefruit juice, and grapefruit zest in a small saucepan over medium heat and bring to a boil. Remove from the heat and whisk it little by little into the eggs, going slowly to temper the eggs and not cook them. Return the mixture to the saucepan and cook, stirring constantly with a wooden spoon, until it reaches 180°F (82°C) on a digital or instant-read thermometer. With a fine-mesh sieve, strain the mixture into the chocolate. Let sit for 1 minute, then whisk from the center to the edges of the bowl, until the crémeux is smooth and homogenous. Pour it in a shallow pan to cool. Once cool enough, place the pan in the refrigerator and let the crémeux set for 2 hours.

Spoon the crémeux into the tartelette shells and top with chocolate curls (see page 158).

Earl Grey Tea–Lavender Ganache Tartelettes

A tartelette filled with ganache never goes out of style. It's traditional and yet always in vogue for many reasons, starting with a universal love for chocolate, and the tart's innate elegance. To add a bit of a surprise, I like to infuse my ganache with tea, in this, the bergamot-scented Earl Grey. You can use fresh or dried lavender—just make sure it's culinary lavender, which means that it has not been treated with pesticides and is safe for consumption. If you grow your own, remove the buds from the stems to measure.

Makes about 30
(1½-inch/4-centimeter) tartelettes

3.5 ounces (100 grams) bittersweet chocolate, finely chopped (about ⅔ cup chopped)

½ cup (120 grams) heavy whipping cream

1½ teaspoons (2 grams) loose Earl Grey tea

¼ teaspoon (0.25 gram) dried culinary lavender buds

1 tablespoon (14 grams) unsalted butter, at room temperature

1 recipe Cocoa Sweet Dough (page 159), prebaked in tartelette shells

Edible gold leaf (optional)

Melt the chocolate over a double boiler. Once it is halfway melted, start stirring it with a heat-resistant spatula until it is completely melted.

Bring the cream to a boil in a small saucepan over medium-high heat. Remove from the heat, stir in the tea and lavender, and let the mixture steep for 5 minutes. With a fine-mesh sieve, strain the mixture into the chocolate and whisk from the center to the edges of the bowl, until the ganache is smooth and homogenous. Whisk in the butter until it is fully incorporated.

Spoon or pipe the ganache into the tartelette shells and let them set in the refrigerator for at least 1 hour. Before serving them, let the filled tartelettes warm up a bit by taking them out of the refrigerator 30 minutes ahead.

If desired, decorate each tartelette with a small piece of gold leaf.

Grand Marnier–Maple-Nut Tortes

The inspiration for these adorable tortes came from working at the Rainbow Room, where we made a "less sweet pecan pie" as a shallow large tart filled with mixed nuts and orange. Here, the orange flavor of the Grand Marnier cuts through the sweetness of the maple syrup. You can use one type of nuts instead of an assortment, if you'd like, but the end result won't be as interesting.

Makes about 18
(2-inch/5-centimeter) tortes

1 recipe Citrus-Pistachio Sweet Dough (page 162), rolled out

1 tablespoon (14 grams) unsalted butter

½ cup (170 grams) pure maple syrup

1 large egg yolk

1 teaspoon (4 grams) pure vanilla extract

1 tablespoon (15 grams) Grand Marnier (or other orange liqueur)

Finely grated zest of ½ orange (4 grams)

¼ teaspoon (1 gram) plus 1 pinch of fine sea salt, divided

5 ounces (about 150 grams) mixed nuts:
pecans, hazelnuts, pistachios, almonds, walnuts,
chopped into ¼-inch (6-millimeter) pieces

1 large egg

1 tablespoon (15 grams) water

Preheat the oven to 350°F (175°C). Arrange one or two (1¾-inch/4.5-centimeter) mini-muffin pans in front of you.

Cut two-thirds of the dough into 18 (2½-inch/6.5-centimeter) circles with a biscuit cutter (these will be your bottom crusts), and the remaining third into 18 (2-inch/5-centimeter) circles with a smaller biscuit cutter (for your top crusts). Keep any dough you are not working with refrigerated. Place the bottom crusts in the bottom of 18 of the mini-muffin pan cavities. Lightly flour your fingertips and press the dough into the cavities. Be careful to not leave air pockets between the dough and the pan.

In a small saucepan, melt the butter, then remove from the heat and stir in the maple syrup, egg yolk, vanilla, Grand Marnier, orange zest, ¼ teaspoon (1 gram) of the salt, and the nuts. Allow to cool for 10 minutes.

In a small bowl, whisk together the egg, water, and pinch of salt. Use a clean pastry brush to brush the egg wash around the perimeter of each shell. Divide the cooled filling evenly in the shells. Place a 2-inch (5-centimeter) top over the filling and pinch the edges together to seal them. Brush the egg wash over the top of each torte; this will help them turn a beautiful golden color. Drag a fork across the dough in a decorative pattern. Bake for 20 minutes and let cool completely before unmolding.

Pineapple-Apple-Cardamom Tortes

Sautéed ripe pineapple with apple is one of my favorite fillings. As pastry chef of Cellar in the Sky, I used it in a phyllo strudel-style dessert. The pineapple adds both sweetness and tartness, for an original twist on an apple pie. Cinnamon would be too expected with apples, while cardamom, which pairs well with pineapple, adds a little *je ne sais quoi*.

Makes about 18
(2-inch/5-centimeter) tortes

1 recipe Coconut Sweet Dough (page 160), rolled out

¼ medium-size ripe pineapple (about 9 ounces/250 grams cut)

1 Granny Smith apple, peeled, halved, and cored

½ vanilla bean

¼ cup (50 grams) granulated sugar

2 tablespoons (28 grams) unsalted butter

¼ teaspoon (0.5 gram) ground cardamom

⅛ teaspoon (0.5 gram) plus 1 pinch of fine sea salt, divided

1 tablespoon (15 grams) Calvados

1 large egg

1 tablespoon (15 grams) water

Preheat the oven to 350°F (175°C). Arrange one or two (1¾-inch/4.5-centimeter) mini-muffin pans in front of you.

Cut two-thirds of the dough into 18 (2½-inch/6.5-centimeter) circles with a biscuit cutter (these will be your bottom crusts), and the remaining third into 18 (2-inch/5-centimeter) circles with a smaller biscuit cutter (for your top crusts). Keep any dough you are not working with refrigerated. Place the bottom crusts in the bottom of 18 of the mini-muffin pan cavities. Lightly flour your fingertips and press the dough into the cavities. Be careful to not leave air pockets between the dough and the pan.

Cut the skin off the pineapple, cut it open, core it, and cut it into ¼-inch (6-millimeter) pieces. Cut the apple into ¼-inch pieces as well.

Split the vanilla bean lengthwise and scrape out the seeds with the back of a paring knife into the sugar. Rub the bean into the sugar to scrape out more vanilla seeds.

Heat a very wide sauté pan (9 to 10 inches [23 to 25 centimeters] in diameter) over medium heat and melt the butter. Add the pineapple, apple, vanilla bean, sugar, cardamom, and ⅛ teaspoon of the salt. Cook, stirring occasionally with a heat-resistant spatula, for about 20 minutes, until the fruit render their juices and the liquid cooks off and becomes slightly translucent. Stir in the Calvados and continue to cook for 1 minute. Remove from the heat and let cool completely before filling tartelette shells. Remove the vanilla bean before filling.

In a small bowl, whisk together the egg, water, and pinch of salt. Use a clean pastry brush to brush the egg wash around the perimeter of each shell. Divide the cooled filling evenly in the shells. Place a 2-inch (5-centimeter) top over the filling and pinch the edges together to seal them. Brush the egg wash over the top of each torte; this will help them turn a beautiful golden color. Drag a fork across the dough in a decorative pattern. Bake for 20 minutes and let cool completely before unmolding.

Apricot-Thyme Tortes

Apricots pair well with herbs. Thyme is widely available so it's an easy choice, but you can experiment here with other fresh herbs, such as tarragon, mint, or rosemary (for the latter, use half the amount of rosemary or it'll be too strong). In the height of the summer, use fresh apricots, but at other times of year canned apricots in syrup will work well.

Makes about 18
(2-inch/5-centimeter) tortes

1 recipe Cornmeal Sweet Dough (page 161), rolled out

½ vanilla bean

½ packed cup (110 grams) light brown sugar

12 ripe apricots, halved and pitted, or 24 canned apricot halves, completely drained

1 packed teaspoon (4 grams) finely grated lemon zest (from 1 lemon)

2 pinches fine sea salt, divided

Leaves from 5 sprigs fresh thyme

1 tablespoons (15 grams) Grand Marnier (or other orange liqueur)

1 large egg

1 tablespoon (15 grams) water

Preheat the oven to 350°F (175°C). Arrange one or two (1¾-inch/4.5-centimeter) mini-muffin pans in front of you.

Cut two-thirds of the dough into 18 (2½-inch/6.5-centimeter) circles with a biscuit cutter (these will be your bottom crusts), and the remaining third into 18 (2-inch/5-centimeter) circles with a smaller biscuit cutter (for your top crusts). Keep any dough you are not working with refrigerated. Place the bottom crusts in the bottom of 18 of the mini-muffin pan cavities. Lightly flour your fingertips and press the dough into the cavities. Be careful to not leave air pockets between the dough and the pan.

Split the vanilla bean lengthwise and scrape out the seeds with the back of a paring knife into the sugar. Rub the bean into the sugar to scrape out more vanilla seeds.

Cut the apricots into ¼-inch (6-millimeter) pieces. Place them with the vanilla bean, sugar, lemon zest, 1 pinch of salt, and thyme in a large sauté pan over medium-high heat. Cook, stirring occasionally with a heat-resistant spatula, for about 8 minutes, until the mixture is bubbly and reaches a jamlike consistency. Stir in the Grand Marnier and continue to cook for 1 minute. Remove from the heat and let cool completely before filling the bottom crusts. Remove the vanilla bean before filling.

In a small bowl, whisk together the egg, water, and the remaining pinch of salt. Use a clean pastry brush to brush the egg wash around the perimeter of the dough. Divide the cooled filling evenly among the crusts. Place a 2-inch (5-centimeter) top over the filling and pinch the edges together to seal them. Brush the egg wash over the top of each torte; this will help them turn a beautiful golden color. Drag a fork across the dough in a decorative pattern. Bake for 20 minutes and let cool completely before unmolding.

Saffron-Raisin-Caramel Tortes

Fleur de sel (its poetic name means "flower of the sea") is a French finishing salt from Brittany. Hand harvested, it is expensive but a little goes a long way flavor-wise. Incorporate finishing salts most effectively after the dish is off the heat.

Makes about 18
(2-inch/5-centimeter) tortes

1 recipe Cornmeal Sweet Dough (page 161) or Vanilla Sweet Dough (page 157), rolled out

⅛ teaspoon loosely measured (1 generous pinch, about 0.5 gram) saffron

¼ cup (60 grams) heavy whipping cream

1 tablespoon (14 grams) unsalted butter

¼ packed cup (55 grams) light brown sugar

1 cup (150 grams) raisins

½ packed teaspoon (2 grams) finely grated orange zest (from ¼ orange)

¼ packed teaspoon (1 gram) finely grated lemon zest (from ¼ lemon)

⅛ teaspoon (1 large pinch) finely diced fresh rosemary

¼ teaspoon (1 gram) fleur de sel

1 large egg

1 tablespoon (15 grams) water

Pinch of salt

Preheat the oven to 350°F (175°C). Arrange one or two (1¾-inch/4.5-centimeter) mini-muffin pans in front of you.

Cut two-thirds of the dough into 18 (2½-inch/6.5-centimeter) circles with a biscuit cutter (these will be your bottom crusts), and the remaining third into 18 (2-inch/5-centimeter) circles with a smaller biscuit cutter (for your top crusts). Keep any dough you are not working with refrigerated. Place the bottom crusts in the bottom of 18 of the mini-muffin pan cavities. Lightly flour your fingertips and press the dough into the cavities. Be careful to not leave air pockets between the dough and the pan.

Crush the saffron with the back of a spoon. Place it in a small microwavable container with the cream and butter and microwave for 1 minute. Pour the mixture into a small saucepan over medium heat and stir in the sugar until it is melted. Stir in the raisins, orange and lemon zests, rosemary, and fleur de sel and cook over medium heat for 5 minutes. Remove from the heat, pour into a shallow pan, and let cool completely.

In a small bowl, whisk together the egg, water and pinch of salt. Use a clean pastry brush to brush the egg wash around the perimeter of each shell. Divide the cooled filling evenly in the shells. Place a 2-inch (5-centimeter) top over the filling and pinch the edges together to seal them. Brush the egg wash over the top of each torte; this will help them turn a beautiful golden color. Drag a fork across the dough in a decorative pattern. Bake for 20 minutes and let cool completely before unmolding.

Lavender-Violet Sablés

SABLÉS

PECAN SABLÉS

CHESTNUT-CINNAMON SABLÉS

CHOCOLATE, SALT, AND PEPPER SABLÉS

CARDAMOM-CITRUS SABLÉS

LAVENDER-VIOLET SABLÉS

THIS QUINTESSENTIAL FRENCH COOKIE RELIES MOSTLY ON USING THE HIGHEST quality butter, to barely hold together its crumbly texture. A European-style butter will have slightly more fat content, which helps give the cookie its characteristic sandy structure. Pick a butter that has a complex flavor, which European styles typically do. Cultured butters are particularly great. Small American producers, especially some cheesemakers, are making those nowadays. All of these sablés bake very quickly. Since the raw dough can be frozen for up to two months, keep a few logs on hand and always be ready to bake a treat for a visiting friend, or get some advance work done on your holiday baking in the early fall.

Pecan Sablés

A sprinkle of fleur de sel tops these rich sablés, which also feature a hint of orange flavor thanks to grated zest in the dough. It's a versatile recipe that goes well with anything from a cup of coffee to a glass of sweet wine.

Makes 20 (1½-inch/4-centimeter) cookies

½ cup (113 grams) good-quality unsalted butter, at room temperature

⅓ cup (60 grams) confectioners' sugar

1 large egg yolk

¾ cup (100 grams) all-purpose flour

¼ cup (33 grams) pecan halves or pieces, finely chopped

⅛ teaspoon (0.5 gram) baking powder

⅛ teaspoon (0.5 gram) fine sea salt

½ packed teaspoon (2 grams) finely grated orange zest (from ¼ orange)

¼ teaspoon (1 gram) fleur de sel

In the bowl of an electric mixer fitted with the paddle attachment, cream the butter and sugar on medium speed until the mixture is smooth, not fluffy, 3 to 5 minutes. Break the egg yolk with a fork and drizzle it in slowly. Stop the mixer and scrape the sides of the bowl, then add the flour, pecans, baking powder, sea salt, and orange zest and mix until just combined, about 30 seconds.

Transfer the dough to a piece of plastic wrap or parchment paper, and use your hands to spread it along the long side of the plastic in a rough log shape. Use the plastic wrap to roll the dough into a 1½-inch (4-centimeter)-wide log, rolling the log on the counter to help even it out and to remove any air pockets. Freeze the dough for 15 minutes, then take it out and round up the shape so it makes as perfect a log as possible. Return to the freezer for 30 minutes. It will keep, frozen and tightly wrapped in two layers of plastic wrap, for up to 2 months.

Preheat the oven to 400°F (200°C) and line a baking sheet with parchment paper.

Remove the dough from the freezer and let it thaw slightly for 5 minutes.

Place the dough on a cutting board and cut it into ⅓-inch (8.5-millimeter)-thick pieces. Roll the log 90 degrees between each cut to keep its shape round. Place the cookies on the baking sheet, leaving ¾ inch (2 centimeters) between them.

Sprinkle an even amount of the fleur de sel on top of each cookie. Bake for 8 to 10 minutes, until the cookies just lift up when you try to move them. Let cool on the baking sheet and serve at room temperature. Store any extra in an airtight container for up to 4 days.

Chestnut-Cinnamon Sablés

The pink peppercorns give these sablés a slight peppery flavor—crush them gently with the back of a spoon. That type of pepper has a very "fresh" and almost flowery flavor, which black pepper would not offer (it would also be too overpowering here, but try it in the chocolate variation pictured at right). Substitute green peppercorns if you must, or omit altogether from the recipe. In season, you can use fresh chestnuts that you cook and peel, but vacuum-packed precooked chestnuts work perfectly, too.

Makes 20
(1½-inch/4-centimeter) cookies

½ cup (113 grams) good-quality unsalted butter, at room temperature

⅓ cup (60 grams) confectioners' sugar

1 large egg yolk

⅔ cup (90 grams) all-purpose flour

⅔ cup (100 grams) whole cooked chestnuts, finely chopped
(see Resources, page 288)

⅛ teaspoon (0.5 gram) pink peppercorns, lightly crushed

⅛ teaspoon (0.5 gram) baking powder

⅛ teaspoon (0.5 gram) fine sea salt

1 tablespoon (12 grams) granulated sugar

½ teaspoon (2 grams) ground cinnamon

¼ teaspoon (1 gram) fleur de sel

In the bowl of an electric mixer fitted with the paddle attachment, cream the butter and sugar on medium speed until the mixture is smooth, not fluffy, 3 to 5 minutes. Break the egg yolk with a fork and drizzle it in slowly. Stop the mixer and scrape the

In the bowl of an electric mixer fitted with the paddle attachment, cream the butter and sugar on medium speed until the mixture is smooth, not fluffy, 3 to 5 minutes. Break the egg yolk with a fork and drizzle it in slowly. Stop the mixer and scrape the sides of the bowl, then add the flour, cardamom, salt, baking powder, and lemon and orange zests, and mix until just combined, about 30 seconds.

Transfer the dough to a piece of plastic wrap or parchment paper, and use your hands to spread it along the long side of the plastic in a rough log shape. Use the plastic wrap to roll the dough into a 1½-inch (4-centimeter)-wide log, rolling the log on the counter to help even it out and to remove any air pockets. Freeze the dough for 15 minutes, then take it out and round up the shape so it makes as perfect a log as possible. Return to the freezer for 30 minutes. It will keep, frozen and tightly wrapped in two layers of plastic wrap, for up to 2 months.

Preheat the oven to 400°F (200°C) and line a baking sheet with parchment paper.

Remove the dough from the freezer and let it thaw slightly for 5 minutes.

Place the dough on a cutting board and cut it into ⅓-inch (8.5-millimeter)-thick pieces. Roll the log 90 degrees between each cut to keep its shape round. Place the cookies on the baking sheet, leaving ¾ inch (2 centimeters) between them.

Bake for 8 to 10 minutes, until the cookies just lift up when you try to move them. Let cool on the baking sheet and serve at room temperature. Store any extra in an airtight container for up to 4 days.

Variation

LAVENDER-VIOLET SABLÉS

Omit the cardamom and lemon, and orange zests. Add ½ teaspoon (0.25 gram) of organic lavender buds when creaming the butter and sugar. Place a small crystallized violet (see Resources, page 288) in the center of each cookie before baking.

Milk Chocolate–Matcha Shortbreads

Shortbreads

SHORTBREADS ARE PERFECT COOKIES FOR THE AFTERNOON, SINCE THEY ARE sturdy enough to be dipped into coffee or tea without disintegrating. They are also great vehicles for a variety of flavors, as you can see here; feel free to further play with your own variations. Because they contain so few ingredients—butter, sugar, and flour—it is important that each of those be of the highest quality. Pick a great-tasting butter, in particular, as you do for sablés (page 187). The two are cousins, but shortbreads are pressed down into a mold and baked, then cut, whereas sablés are rolled into logs, chilled, and then sliced and baked. Shortbreads are simpler to make, as a result—so simple that the first thing kids should learn to bake. Since they easily freeze and have an indulgent, rich texture, make plenty ahead of time for special occasions or brunches.

Orange-Rosemary Shortbreads

I usually bake this recipe in a round cake pan, but you can use a square or loaf pan just as easily. With so few ingredients, the flavors of orange and rosemary shine through; I like to serve these shortbreads with vanilla ice cream.

Makes 16 wedges

¾ cup (170 grams) good-quality unsalted butter, at room temperature

⅓ cup plus 1 teaspoon (84 grams) granulated sugar, divided

½ teaspoon (0.5 gram) finely chopped fresh rosemary

Finely grated zest of 1 orange

1⅓ cups (180 grams) all-purpose flour

½ teaspoon (2 grams) fine sea salt, divided

Preheat the oven to 300°F (150°C).

In the bowl of an electric mixer fitted with the paddle attachment, cream the butter, ⅓ cup (80 grams) of the sugar, rosemary, and orange zest on medium speed until the mixture becomes pale and fluffy, 5 to 10 minutes. Add the flour and ¼ teaspoon (1 gram) of the salt and mix until just combined, about 30 seconds.

Press the dough down into a 9-inch (23-centimeter) round cake or pie pan lined with two crisscrossing sheets of parchment paper (see page 200). It should be about ½ inch (1.25 centimeters) thick.

Stir together the remaining 1 teaspoon (4 grams) of the sugar and ¼ teaspoon (1 gram) of the salt. Sprinkle over the top of the shortbread.

Bake for 30 to 35 minutes, or until the shortbread feels firm when you touch it and it pulls slightly from the edges of the pan.

Remove from the oven and cut into 16 wedges while the shortbread is warm. Store at room temperature in an airtight container for up to 4 days or in the freezer, well wrapped in plastic wrap, for up to 2 months.

CUTTING SHORTBREAD

Line the pan with two sheets of crisscrossing parchment paper, which will allow you to lift the whole shortbread out of the pan once baked and cut.

Shortbread is less crumbly if cut while warm, just out of the oven. To cut shortbreads into even slices, use a dough scraper. It will cut from the edge of the pan to the center and, unlike a knife, will not dull from metal-to-metal contact.

Ginger-Coconut-Lime Shortbreads

This recipe takes on tropical flavors with ginger, coconut, and lime. This unexpected combination for shortbread evokes a sunny island where the only tea—my favorite companion for shortbread—you'd drink would come with lots of ice, and maybe some rum. Try it with a ginger or green tea here.

Makes 16 wedges

¾ cup (170 grams) good-quality unsalted butter, at room temperature

⅓ cup plus 1 teaspoon (84 grams) granulated sugar, divided

½ cup (75 grams) candied crystallized ginger, finely chopped

¼ cup (25 grams) sweetened flaked coconut

Finely grated zest of 1 lime

1⅓ cups (180 grams) all-purpose flour

¼ teaspoon (1 gram) fine sea salt

⅛ teaspoon (0.5 grams) ground ginger

Preheat the oven to 300°F (150°C).

In the bowl of an electric mixer fitted with the paddle attachment, cream the butter, ⅓ cup (80 grams) of the sugar, crystallized ginger, coconut, and lime zest on medium speed until the mixture becomes pale and fluffy, 5 to 10 minutes. Add the flour and salt and mix until just combined, about 30 seconds.

Press the dough down into a 9-inch (23-centimeter) round cake or pie pan lined with two crisscrossing sheets of parchment paper (see page 200). It should be about ½ inch (1.25 centimeters) thick.

Stir together the remaining 1 teaspoon (4 grams) of sugar and the ginger. Sprinkle over the top of the shortbread.

Bake for 30 to 35 minutes, until the shortbread feels firm when you touch it and it pulls slightly from the edges of the pan.

Remove from the oven and cut into 16 wedges while the shortbread is warm. Store at room temperature in an airtight container for up to 4 days or in the freezer, well wrapped in plastic wrap, for up to 2 months.

Chocolate-Macadamia Shortbreads

Chocolate pairs well with most nuts, so play with this recipe using peanuts or cashews, for example. The salt balances the chocolate and makes the shortbread less sweet.

Makes 16 (2-inch/5-centimeter) squares

¾ cup (170 grams) good-quality unsalted butter, at room temperature

⅓ cup plus 1 teaspoon (84 grams) granulated sugar, divided

1⅓ cups (180 grams) all-purpose flour

½ cup (75 grams) salted macadamias, finely chopped

2.7 ounces (75 grams) bittersweet chocolate, finely chopped (about ½ cup chopped)

¼ teaspoon (1 gram) fine sea salt

⅛ teaspoon (0.5 gram) fleur del sel

Preheat the oven to 300°F (150°C).

In the bowl of an electric mixer fitted with the paddle attachment, cream the butter and sugar on medium speed until the mixture becomes pale and fluffy, for 5 to 10 minutes. Add the flour, macadamias, chocolate, and ¼ teaspoon (1 gram) of the salt and mix until just combined, about 30 seconds.

Press the dough down into an 8-inch (20-centimeter) square pan lined with two crisscrossing sheets of parchment paper (see page 200). It should be about ½ inch (1.25 centimeters) thick.

Stir together the remaing 1 teaspoon of sugar and the fleur de sel. Sprinkle over the top of the shortbread.

Bake for 30 to 35 minutes, until the shortbread feels firm when you touch it and it pulls slightly from the edges of the pan.

Remove from the oven and cut into 2-inch (5-centimeter) squares while the shortbread is warm. Store at room temperature in an airtight container for up to 4 days or in the freezer, well wrapped in plastic wrap, for up to 2 months.

Variation

CHOCOLATE-CHILE SHORTBREADS

Omit the nuts. Add ½ teaspoon (2 grams) of ancho chile powder with the butter.

Variation

MILK CHOCOLATE–MATCHA SHORTBREADS

Omit the nuts. Add 1 teaspoon (2 grams) of matcha powder with the flour. Substitute milk chocolate for the bittersweet.

Chai Langues de Chat with Blueberry Cream Filling

Tea Cookies

APRICOT-STRAWBERRY LINZER COOKIES

CHAI LANGUES DE CHAT WITH BLUEBERRY CREAM FILLING

SESAME-CHOCOLATE-ORANGE WAFERS WITH ORANGE GANACHE

CRANBERRY PALETS WITH APRICOT-RUM GLAZE

MY FAMILY MOVED TO AUSTRALIA WHEN I WAS A CHILD, AND THEN TO ENGLAND during my high school years, so the time I spent living in those countries partly explains why I love both tea and any treat that goes with it so much. The cookies in this chapter all have in common that they are perfect accompaniments for a cup of hot tea, and that they are inspired by where I have learned and worked in the past. In pastry school, my teacher Mark Ramsdell introduced us to classic langues de chat and palets aux raisins; the sandwiched sesame wafers are adapted from chocolate chip wafers we made at the Rainbow Room, and the mini Linzer cookies combine my two favorite flavors for the jam "window."

Apricot-Strawberry Linzer Cookies

Linzer cookies traditionally are made with hazelnut flour, as is the case here. You can grind hazelnuts into a fine powder or purchase the flour; Bob's Red Mill is a nationally available brand. Some stores carry frozen fruit purées (Kalustyan's in New York, for example), but ordering them online might be the best way to get them otherwise (see Resources, page 288). If you prefer to use store-bought jam(s), you will need about 1 cup. Apricot and strawberries are two of my favorite fruits, but of course you can make this recipe with your own preferred jam.

Makes 36 (1¾-inch/4.5-centimeter) cookies, or 18 sandwiches

COOKIES

4 tablespoons (56 grams) unsalted butter, at room temperature

½ cup (90 grams) confectioners' sugar

1 large egg

½ teaspoon (2 grams) pure vanilla extract

1 cup (135 grams) all-purpose flour, plus more for dusting

½ cup (54 grams) hazelnut flour (see Resources, page 288)

¼ teaspoon (1 gram) fine sea salt

APRICOT-STRAWBERRY JAM

½ cup (160 grams) apricot purée or canned apricots, well drained and puréed in a food processor

¼ cup (75 grams) strawberry purée or fresh or frozen and thawed strawberries, puréed in a food processor

¼ cup (50 grams) granulated sugar

½ teaspoon (2.5 grams) freshly squeezed and strained lemon juice (from ½ lemon)

⅛ cup (19 grams) confectioners' sugar, for dusting

MAKE THE COOKIES: In the bowl of an electric mixer fitted with the paddle attachment, cream the butter and confectioners' sugar on medium speed until the mixture becomes pale and fluffy, 5 to 10 minutes. Gradually incorporate the egg, then the vanilla. Add the 1 cup all-purpose flour, hazelnut flour, and salt and mix until just combined, about 30 seconds.

Transfer the dough to a lightly floured piece of parchment paper, dust it lightly with flour, and roll it out until it is ⅛ inch (3 millimeters) thick. Refrigerate the dough for 30 minutes.

Using a 1¾-inch (4.5-centimeter) cookie cutter, cut 36 cookies into the dough. With a 1-inch (2.5-centimeter) cookie cutter, cut out a hole in half of the cookies; they will be the tops of the cookies. Return the cut-out dough to the refrigerator for 30 minutes.

Preheat the oven to 375°F (190°C) and line two baking sheets with parchment paper.

With an offset spatula, transfer the bottom and top cookies to the prepared baking sheets. Bake for 5 minutes, until the cookies are golden around the edges. Remove from the oven and let cool on the baking sheet.

MAKE THE JAM: Heat the apricot and strawberry purées and the granulated sugar in a medium nonreactive saucepan over medium-high heat, stirring constantly with a heat-resistant spatula. Clip a calibrated candy thermometer to the pan and continue to cook the mixture, stirring constantly, until it reaches 217°F (103°C) or clings to the spatula, about 10 minutes. The jam will thicken considerably as it cools, so be careful to not overcook or caramelize it. Remove from the heat, stir in the lemon juice, quickly pour the jam into a shallow pan, and refrigerate until completely cool. The jam will keep in an airtight container in the refrigerator for up to 1 month.

ASSEMBLE THE COOKIES: Place the confectioners' sugar in a small fine-mesh strainer and dust the top cookies (the ones with the cut-out holes).

Spoon the jam into a piping bag fitted with a ½-inch (1.25-centimeter) round tip (alternatively, cut a ½-inch opening in the bag). Pipe a 1½-inch (4-centimeter)-wide circle of jam on the bottom cookie. Place a top cookie over the jam. Store the Linzer cookies in an airtight container at room temperature for up to 2 days.

Chai Langues de Chat with Blueberry Cream Filling

Langues de chat are delicate cookies that break easily, and also absorb humidity; eat them the same day you fill them. You can use a neutral honey, such as clover, but the spices can also take something stronger if you prefer baking with a more assertive honey. To grind the tea, pulse your favorite black tea in a spice or coffee grinder until it reaches a fine texture. If necessary, first clean the grinder by pulsing a bit of white rice, which will get rid of lingering coffee flavor. You can also use a mortar and pestle. To cut down the sometimes overwhelming sweetness of white chocolate, I like using Opalys, a low-sugar-added variety made by Valrhona. These cookies are great on their own, but you can also sandwich them with your favorite ganache recipe, or as suggested here, with a blueberry cream filling.

Makes about 50 (3-inch/7.5-centimeter-long) cookies or 25 sandwiches

COOKIES

2 tablespoons (36 grams) honey

1 teaspoon (1 gram) finely ground black tea

6 tablespoons (84 grams) unsalted butter, at room temperature

½ cup (90 grams) confectioners' sugar

3 large egg whites

½ cup (68 grams) all-purpose flour

¼ cup (28 grams) cake flour

½ teaspoon (1.5 grams) ground ginger

½ teaspoon (2 grams) ground cinnamon

½ teaspoon (1 gram) ground cardamom

⅛ teaspoon (2 pinches) ground cloves

⅛ teaspoon (2 pinches) freshly ground black pepper

FILLING

½ cup (120 grams) blueberry purée (see Resources, page 288) or fresh blueberries (boil for 1 minute and purée with an immersion blender)

¼ teaspoon (1 gram) ground cinnamon

8.8 ounces (250 grams) white chocolate finely chopped, preferably Opalys (about 1⅔ cups)

MAKE THE COOKIES: Preheat the oven to 400°F (200°C) and line a baking sheet with parchment paper.

Heat the honey and tea in a small saucepan over medium heat until the honey begins to boil, then remove from the heat and let the mixture cool completely.

In the bowl of an electric mixer fitted with the paddle attachment, cream the butter and sugar on medium speed until the mixture is pale and fluffy, 5 to 10 minutes.

Stir the egg whites into the honey mixture.

In a medium bowl, stir together the all-purpose and cake flours, ginger, cinnamon, cardamom, cloves, and pepper. Alternating between the flour and the honey mixtures, add the dry and wet ingredients to the mixer a little at a time, only mixing until just combined before adding more. Begin and end with the dry ingredients.

Spoon the batter into a piping bag fitted with a ½-inch (1.25-centimeter) round tip (alternatively, cut a ½-inch opening in the bag). Pipe the batter into 3-inch (7.5-centimeter)-long ovals (cat tongues) on the baking sheet, 1 inch (2.5 centimeters) apart, until the batter is used up. If not all cookies fit on the prepared baking sheet, keep the batter in the bag until the first batch has baked, or use a second lined baking sheet.

Bake for 7 minutes, until the cookies are golden around the edges. Remove from the oven and let cool on the baking sheet. The baked cookies, without filling, can keep in an airtight container at room temperature for up to 2 days.

MAKE THE FILLING: Heat the blueberry purée and cinnamon in a small saucepan over medium-high heat and bring to a rapid boil. Boil for 5 minutes. Remove from the heat, pour in the chopped chocolate, and shake the pot so that the chocolate is submerged. Let sit for 1 minute, then whisk rapidly from the center of the pot outward in a spiral shape until the chocolate is fully melted. Pour the mixture into a shallow pan and refrigerate to let it set, about 1 hour.

When the mixture is firm, spoon the filling into a piping bag fitted with a ¼-inch (6-millimeter) round tip (alternatively, cut a ¼-inch opening in the bag). Pipe a strip of filling over the length of one cookie, and top it with another, slightly pressing the top cookie so that the sandwich is tight. Once filled, eat them the same day.

Sesame-Chocolate-Orange Wafers with Orange Ganache

I typically chop chocolate in a food processor; it's more to clean, but it helps ensure that the chocolate pieces are chopped finely enough for a small amount of chocolate to melt without lumps. If you chose to do that here, first chop the chocolate for the ganache, set it aside, and then chop the two chocolates used in the cookies together. The chopped pieces should measure about ⅛ inch (3 millimeters). Sesame and orange are two flavors that individually complement chocolate. Combining them makes for an even more powerful flavor team.

Makes about 80 (1¾-inch/4.5-centimeter) cookies, or 40 sandwiches

COOKIES

½ cup (112 grams) unsalted butter, at room temperature

⅔ cup (133 grams) granulated sugar

½ packed teaspoon (2 grams) finely grated orange zest (from ¼ orange)

1 large egg

½ teaspoon (2 grams) pure vanilla extract

½ cup (58 grams) cake flour

1.8 ounces (50 grams) bittersweet chocolate, finely chopped (about ⅓ cup chopped)

1.3 ounces (38 grams) white chocolate, finely chopped (about ¼ cup chopped)

3 tablespoons (30 grams) white sesame seeds

1 tablespoon (10 grams) black sesame seeds

¼ teaspoon (1 gram) fine sea salt

GANACHE

½ cup (120 grams) heavy whipping cream

½ packed teaspoon (2 grams) finely grated orange zest (from ¼ orange)

4 ounces (113 grams) semisweet chocolate, finely chopped (about ¾ cup chopped)

MAKE THE COOKIES: Preheat the oven to 375°F (190°C) and line a baking sheet with parchment paper.

In the bowl of an electric mixer fitted with the paddle attachment, cream the butter, sugar, and orange zest on medium speed until the mixture becomes pale and fluffy, 5 to 10 minutes.

With a fork, whisk the egg into a bowl to break it up. Reduce the mixer speed to low and let the egg and vanilla trickle into the mixture. Once incorporated, add the flour, chocolatse, sesame seeds, and salt, and mix until just combined, about 30 seconds.

Spoon the batter into a piping bag fitted with a ½-inch (1.25-centimeter) round tip (alternatively, cut a ½-inch opening in the bag). Pipe the batter into 1½-inch (4-centimeter) mounds on the baking sheet, 1 inch (2.5 centimeters) apart, until the batter is used up. If not all cookies fit on the prepared baking sheet, keep the batter in the bag until the first batch has baked, or use a second lined baking sheet.

Bake for 6 minutes, until the cookies are golden around the edges. Remove from the oven and let cool completely on the baking sheet.

MAKE THE GANACHE: Heat the cream and orange zest in a small saucepan over medium-high heat and bring to a boil. Remove from the heat, pour in the chopped chocolate, and shake the pot so that the chocolate is submerged. Let sit for 1 minute, then whisk rapidly from the center of the pot outward in a spiral shape until the chocolate is fully melted and the ganache is emulsified. Pour the mixture into a shallow pan and refrigerate to let it set, about 1 hour.

When the mixture is firm, spoon the batter into a piping bag fitted with a ½-inch (1.25-centimeter) round tip (alternatively, cut a ½-inch opening in the bag). Pipe a 1½-inch (4-centimeter) mound at the center of one cookie and top it with another, slightly twisting the top cookie so that the sandwich is tight. Store the sandwiched cookies in an airtight container in the refrigerator for up to 2 days.

Cranberry Palets with Apricot-Rum Glaze

Cranberries are a particularly American twist on this very French cookie, typically made with raisins. Feel free to use those instead, or even dried blueberries or finely chopped dried cherries. Likewise, play with the glaze: You can use any type of preserve you'd like; if it is chunky, strain it after you heat it.

Makes about 60
(2-inch/5-centimeter) cookies

COOKIES

2 tablespoons plus 2 teaspoons (38 grams) unsalted butter, at room temperature

¼ cup (50 grams) granulated sugar

1 large egg

½ teaspoon (2 grams) pure vanilla extract

⅓ cup (45 grams) all-purpose flour

¼ cup (33 grams) finely chopped dried cranberries

GLAZE

2 tablespoons (59 grams) apricot preserves

1 tablespoon (15 grams) dark rum

MAKE THE COOKIES: Preheat the oven to 400°F (200°C) and line a baking sheet with parchment paper.

In the bowl of an electric mixer fitted with the paddle attachment, cream the butter and sugar on medium speed until the mixture becomes pale and fluffy, 5 to 10 minutes. Gradually incorporate the egg, then the vanilla. Add the flour and cranberries and mix until just combined, about 30 seconds.

Spoon the batter into a piping bag fitted with a ½-inch (1.25-centimeter) round tip (alternatively, cut a ½-inch opening in the bag). Pipe the batter into 1½-inch (4-centimeter) mounds on the baking sheet, 1 inch (2.5 centimeters) apart, until the batter is used up. If not all cookies fit on the prepared baking sheet, keep the batter in the bag until the first batch has baked, or use a second lined baking sheet.

Bake for 6 minutes, until the cookies are golden around the edges. Remove from the oven and let cool completely on the baking sheet.

MAKE THE GLAZE: Heat the apricot preserves in a microwave-safe bowl or in a small saucepan over medium heat until they are barely fluid. With a pastry brush, brush the glaze on the cooled cookies.

Stir the rum into the confectioners' sugar in a small owl. Drizzle on the cookies in a decorative pattern. Let the glaze dry before stacking the cookies. Store them in an airtight container for up to 3 days at room temperature. You can place a sheet of waxed paper in between each layer to make sure they don't stick together.

Carrot Cake Petits Fours

Petits Fours Glacés

WHITE CHOCOLATE–
SALTED CARAMEL PETITS FOURS

COCONUT-TAMARIND–
PASSION FRUIT PETITS FOURS

CARROT CAKE PETITS FOURS

These glazed and iced petits fours are classic and elegant, perfect for showers or a fancy brunch. While each step is easy to accomplish, they are among the most labor-intensive recipes in this book. It's well worth the effort for a special occasion, such as an anniversary brunch, baby shower, or bridal luncheon. Many elements can also be made ahead of time. You can decorate the tops for various seasonal occasions, such as with spiderweb patterns on the white chocolate for a Halloween buffet or flowers in the spring. To easily transport them, place them in cupcake liners.

You will need quarter-sheet pans (13 x 9 inches [33 x 23 centimeters]), which are easily available online and will be versatile in your kitchen beyond these petits fours, including to help you organize your ingredients at the start of a recipe. If you prefer to bake the cakes in half-sheet pans, you'll need to cut them into two even halves. If you have only one quarter-sheet pan, divide the batter in half and bake the cakes one at a time. A pretty glaze protects the moist cake and gives it shelf life. Some people think that petits fours are dated, but it's mostly because most of the ones available are overly sweet and drowned in fondants, or just plain bad. These recipes here are made for twenty-first-century palates, with innovative flavor combinations.

PERFECT SQUARES

To cleanly cut each petit four dip the top third tip of a chef's knife into very hot water and carefully dry it off on a clean towel.

White Chocolate–Salted Caramel Petits Fours

Chocolate and caramel often appear together, as a sweet power couple. The caramel here is made with goat's milk, which gives it a slight tanginess and a more complex flavor than cow's milk would. The salt cuts through the sweetness.

The weight of goat's milk varies based on lots of factors, including the goats' diet. You will obtain the most consistent result for this recipe by using the US liquid volume measurements, or 2 cups. If you overreduce the goat's milk and need to top it off but have run out, it's fine to use cow's milk.

The order of assembly for these petits fours is white chocolate cake, salted goat caramel crémeux, white chocolate cake, and semisweet chocolate glaze.

Makes 24 (2 x 1¼-inch/5 x 3-centimeter) petits fours

WHITE CHOCOLATE CAKE

Vegetable oil cooking spray

2.7 ounces (75 grams) white chocolate, finely chopped (about ½ cup chopped)

4 tablespoons (56 grams) unsalted butter, cut into 1-inch (2.5-centimeter) cubes

1⅓ cups (180 grams) all-purpose flour

½ cup (100 grams) granulated sugar

2 teaspoons (8 grams) baking powder

½ teaspoon (2 grams) fine sea salt

4 large egg whites

1 teaspoon (4 grams) pure vanilla extract

1 cup (246 grams) buttermilk

FOR ASSEMBLY

Salted Goat Caramel Crémeux (recipe follows)

Semisweet Chocolate Glaze (see page 152)

Gold leaf dust (optional)

MAKE THE CAKE: Preheat the oven to 350°F (175°C). Spray two quarter-sheet (13 x 9-inch/33 x 23-centimeter) pans with vegetable oil cooking spray and line them with parchment paper.

Using the method on page 18, melt the chocolate over a double boiler, then set aside.

In the bowl of an electric mixer fitted with the paddle attachment, mix the butter, flour, sugar, baking powder, and salt on medium speed until the mixture is homogenous and resembles cornmeal, with no visible chunks of butter.

In a small bowl, whisk together the egg whites and vanilla. Reduce the mixer speed to low and add one-third of the egg white mixture. Increase the speed to medium and beat for 1 minute until everything is incorporated. Stop the mixer, scrape down the sides of the bowl, and repeat the procedure 2 more times until all of the egg whites are incorporated.

Whisk the buttermilk into the melted chocolate until well combined. With the mixer on low speed, drizzle the mixture into the bowl. Increase the speed to medium and beat the mixture for 1 minute, until combined.

Divide the batter evenly between the two sheet pans and spread it so the top is even. Bake for about 15 minutes, until the cakes puff up in the middle and a skewer inserted in the middle comes out clean. Let them cool completely.

TO ASSEMBLE THE PETITS FOURS: Place a sheet of parchment paper on a half-sheet pan and a wire rack on top of the paper. Put a 12-inch (30-centimeter) cake cardboard at the center of the wire rack and invert one layer of cake over it. Soften the crémeux by stirring it with a spatula, then spread it evenly over the cake. Place the second layer of cake on top of the crémeux.

To glaze the tops of the cakes only: Warm the chocolate glaze to 50°F (10°C) over a double boiler (see page 18). Flood (completely cover) the top of the cake with the glaze, quickly using an offset spatula to spread it as necessary. Tap the glazing tray to level out the glaze. Refrigerate for about 45 minutes, to let the glaze set.

Trim about ½ inch (1.25 centimeters) off the sides of the cake with a chef's knife, to even them out. Using a ruler for guidance and a chef's knife, cut the cakes into 6 even strips lengthwise and 4 even strips widthwise. You should have 24 (2 x 1¼-inch/5 x 3-centimeter) rectangles. Use a small offset spatula to remove the cakes from the glazing rack. Decorate with a gold leaf, if desired.

Alternatively, you can glaze each individual cake: Trim about ½ inch (1.25 centimeters) off the sides of the cake with a serrated knife, to even them out. Using a ruler for guidance and a serrated knife, cut the cakes into 6 even strips lengthwise and 4 even strips widthwise. You should have 24 (2 x 1¼-inch/5 x 3-centimeter) rectangles. Use a small offset spatula to remove the cakes from the cardboard.

Remove the cardboard, then place the cakes on the rack, spaced about 1 inch (2.5 centimeters) apart.

Warm the chocolate glaze to 50°F (10°C) over a double boiler (see page 18). Spoon the glaze into a piping bag and cut a ¼-inch (6-millimeter) opening straight across the tip of the pastry bag. Pipe the glaze so that it completely covers the top and sides of each cake. Scrape up the glaze that falls on the parchment paper and put it back into the piping bag until all the cakes are glazed. Tap the glazing tray to level out the glaze. Refrigerate for about 45 minutes, to let the glaze set. Use a small offset spatula to remove the cakes from the glazing rack. Decorate with gold leaf dust, if desired.

SALTED GOAT CARAMEL CRÉMEUX

Makes about 1 cup (227 grams)

2 cups (about 488 grams) goat's milk (see headnote, page 225)

⅛ packed cup (28 grams) dark brown sugar

⅛ teaspoon (0.5 gram) baking soda

1¼ sheets (2.5 grams) gold gelatin (see page 20)

2 cups (460 grams) ice water

1.8 ounces (50 grams) white chocolate, finely chopped (about ⅓ cup chopped)

¼ teaspoon (1 gram) fleur de sel

4 large egg yolks

¼ cup (60 grams) heavy whipping cream

Heat the goat's milk in a medium saucepan over medium heat and let it reduce by slightly more than half of its volume, which should take about 30 minutes. You should have about ¾ cup (183 grams) milk. If you reduce it too much and end up with less than that, make up the difference by adding more milk. Whisk in the sugar and baking soda and clip a calibrated candy thermometer to the pot. Stir constantly with a heat-resistant spatula and cook the mixture to continue reducing it, until it reaches 200°F (93°C). Remove the caramelized goat's milk from the heat and set aside.

Soften the gelatin in the ice water for 3 minutes, then strain out the excess liquid through a fine-mesh strainer. Place the hydrated gelatin, chocolate, and fleur de sel in a medium bowl.

In a heat-resistant medium bowl, whisk the egg yolks until combined. Heat the cream and caramelized goat's milk in a small saucepan over medium heat and bring to a boil. Remove the mixture from the heat and whisk it little by little into the eggs, going slowly to temper the eggs and not cook them. Return the mixture to the pan and cook, stirring constantly with a wooden spoon, until it reaches 180°F (82°C) on a digital or instant-read thermometer. With a fine-mesh sieve, strain the mixture into the chocolate. Let sit for 1 minute, then whisk from the center to the edges of the bowl, until the crémeux is smooth and homogenous. Pour it into a shallow pan to cool. Once cool enough, place the pan in the refrigerator and let the crémeux set for 2 hours.

Coconut-Tamarind-Passion Fruit Petits Fours

Tamarind is popular in Asian and Latin sweets, which is why I like to pair it with coconut and passion fruit here, for a completely different flavor profile from what might be considered typically French or American. It is tart and often has a slightly fibrous texture. If you buy tamarind paste with seeds, you'll have to remove the seeds with your fingers—they are the size of date seeds, roughly, so easy to spot. You might sometimes find liquid tamarind paste concentrate, which is not the right product either. Asian and Latin grocery stores, in addition to online sources, stock the kind of seedless tamarind paste you need here.

The order of assembly for these petits fours is coconut cake, tamarind jam, coconut cake, and passion fruit fondant.

Makes 24 (2 x 1¼-inch/5 x 3-centimeter) petits fours

COCONUT CAKE

Vegetable oil cooking spray

½ cup (112 grams) unsalted butter

¾ cup (150 grams) granulated sugar

1⅓ cups (180 grams) all-purpose flour

1½ teaspoons (6 grams) baking powder

¼ teaspoon (1 gram) fine sea salt

3 large egg whites

1 cup (250 grams) unsweetened coconut milk

½ teaspoon (2 grams) pure vanilla extract

FOR ASSEMBLY

Tamarind Jam (recipe follows)

Passion Fruit Fondant (recipe follows)

MAKE THE CAKE: Preheat the oven to 350°F (175°C). Spray two quarter-sheet (13 x 9-inch/33 x 23-centimeter) pans with vegetable oil cooking spray and line them with parchment paper.

In the bowl of an electric mixer fitted with the paddle attachment, cream the butter and sugar on medium speed until the mixture is pale and fluffy, 5 to 10 minutes.

In a medium bowl, whisk together the flour, baking powder, and salt. In another medium bowl, whisk together the egg whites, coconut milk, and vanilla.

With the mixer running, alternately incorporate the dry and the wet ingredients into the butter mixture, starting and ending with the flour mixture. Mix until the batter is just combined, about 30 seconds.

Divide the batter evenly between the two sheet pans and spread it so the top is even. Bake for about 12 minutes, until the cakes puff up in the middle and a skewer inserted in the middle comes out clean. Let them cool completely.

TO ASSEMBLE THE PETITS FOURS: Place a sheet of parchment paper on a half-sheet pan and a wire rack on top of the paper. Put a 12-inch (30-centimeter) cake cardboard at the center of the wire rack and invert one layer of cake over it. Soften the tamarind jam by stirring it with a spatula, then spread it evenly over the cake. Place the second layer of cake on top of the jam.

Adjust the consistency of the passion fruit fondant to a glaze until it is opaque and fluid (see page 234). Set aside 2 tablespoons of the fondant in a small bowl. Flood (completely cover) the top of the cake with the fondant, quickly using an offset spatula to spread it as necessary. Tap the glazing tray to level out the fondant.

Color the reserved fondant with a few drops of yellow food coloring (liquid, paste, or gel coloring works). Spoon it into a pastry bag and cut just the tip of the bag, to make a small opening. Drizzle the darker fondant quickly over the top of the cakes as desired to decorate them. Let the fondant set at room temperature for about 45 minutes.

Trim about ½ inch (1.25 centimeters) off the sides of the cake with a chef's knife to even them out. Using a ruler for guidance and a chef's knife, cut the cakes into 6 even strips lengthwise and 4 even strips widthwise. You should have 24 (2 x 1¼-inch/5 x 3-centimeter) rectangles. Use a small offset spatula to remove the petits fours from the cardboard and place them into small paper cupcake liners.

TAMARIND JAM

Makes about 1 cup (227 grams)

1 cup (280 grams) seedless tamarind paste

½ cup (100 grams) granulated sugar

Place the tamarind paste and sugar in a small saucepan over medium-low heat and stir constantly with a heat-resistant spatula until the mixture thickens, about 8 minutes. To test that it is ready, dip the heat-resistant spatula into the mixture and let it drip onto a plate. The drop should have the consistency of a thick jam. You can also clip a calibrated candy thermometer to the pan; the jam will be ready when it reaches approximately 220°F (104°C).

Remove the jam from the heat, pour it into a shallow pan, and let it cool. It will further thicken as it cools.

PASSION FRUIT FONDANT

Makes 1¾ cups (570 grams)

2½ cups (500 grams) granulated sugar

¾ cup (180 grams) passion fruit purée or juice (see Resources, page 288)

½ cup (85 grams) light corn syrup

½ teaspoon (2 grams) fine sea salt

1 to 3 drops yellow liquid, paste, or gel food coloring, plus more as desired for assembly

Place the sugar in a medium saucepan, then slowly and carefully pour the passion fruit purée in a spiral motion from the edges of the pan to its center, without moving the pan. Add the corn syrup and salt. Clip a calibrated candy thermometer to the pan and cook over medium heat until the sugar reaches 237°F (114°C). If the sugar is not all dissolved as it cooks, stir it gently and clean any crystals that form on the sides of the pan with a pastry brush dipped in water.

Once ready, pour the fondant into the bowl of an electric mixer, insert the thermometer into it, and let it cool at room temperature until it reaches 120°F (49°C), without stirring. Set the mixer with the paddle attachment, add the food coloring to the fondant, and beat it on medium-low speed for about 25 minutes, until it turns into a thick and opaque paste. Use immediately.

TO USE THE FONDANT: Check a bit with a spoon—the fondant should have the fluidity of a ganache and be opaque. It should coat the back of the spoon to the point that you no longer see the wood or metal. If necessary, add a few drops of water at a time to thin it out. If you add too much water, you risk overthinning the fondant, which may cause drips as you dip. When the fondant is correctly thinned out, it should cover a cake without being so thin as to be translucent or so thick as to pile up.

Carrot Cake Petits Fours

In France and the United States, carrot cake remains a classic. This version, which includes Grand Marnier and is topped with orange fondant, is on the fancier side of the genre, but well worth it. It's a great recipe for a spring party, or in the late summer when carrots abound at the farmers' market and are at their most flavorful peak.

The order of assembly for these petits fours is carrot cake, white chocolate–cream cheese filling, carrot cake, and orange fondant.

Makes 24 (2 x 1¼-inch/5 x 3-centimeter) petits fours

CARROT CAKE

Vegetable oil cooking spray

1 large ripe fresh apricot (80 grams), halved, pitted, and chopped, or 2 canned apricot halves, well drained

½ cup raisins (40 grams)

Juice of ½ orange (90 grams)

1 tablespoon (15 grams) Grand Marnier

2 large eggs

⅔ cup (140 grams) vegetable oil

1 teaspoon (4 grams) pure vanilla extract

1 large carrot (290 grams), peeled and grated

1 cup (130 grams) pecan halves or pieces, roughly chopped

1 cup (135 grams) all-purpose flour

¾ cup (150 grams) granulated sugar

¾ teaspoon (3 grams) baking powder

½ teaspoon (2 grams) ground cinnamon

¼ teaspoon (1 gram) fine sea salt

1 pinch (1 gram) ground cardamom

1 pinch (1 gram) ground nutmeg

FOR ASSEMBLY

White Chocolate–Cream Cheese Filling (recipe follows)

Orange Fondant (recipe follows)

MAKE THE CAKE: Preheat the oven to 350°F (175°C). Spray two quarter-sheet (13 x 9-inch/33 x 23-centimeter) pans with vegetable oil cooking spray and line them with parchment paper.

Place the apricot pieces and raisins in a small bowl. Pour the orange juice and Grand Marnier over them and let macerate for about 10 minutes.

In a large bowl whisk the eggs to break them up and stir in the oil and vanilla. Stir in the carrots, pecans, and apricot mixture. Stir in the flour, sugar, baking powder, cinnamon, salt, cardamom, and nutmeg until just combined, about 30 seconds.

Divide the batter evenly between the two sheet pans and spread it so the top is even. Bake for about 20 minutes, until the cakes puff up in the middle and a skewer inserted in the middle comes out clean. Let them cool completely.

TO ASSEMBLE THE PETITS FOURS: Place a sheet of parchment paper on a half-sheet pan and a wire rack on top of the paper. Put a 12-inch (30-centimeter) cake cardboard at the center of the wire rack and invert one layer of cake over it. Soften the white chocolate–cream cheese filling by stirring it with a spatula, then spread it evenly over the cake. Place the second layer of cake on top of the filling.

Adjust the consistency of the orange fondant to a glaze until it is opaque and fluid (see next page). Flood (completely cover) the top of the cake with the fondant, quickly using an offset spatula to spread it as necessary. Tap the glazing tray to level out the fondant and let set at room temperature for about 45 minutes.

Trim about ½ inch (1.25 centimeters) off the sides of the cake with a serrated knife to even them out. Using a ruler for guidance and a chef's knife, cut the cakes into 6 even strips lengthwise and 4 even strips widthwise. You should have 24 (2 x 1¼-inch/ 5 x 3-centimeter) rectangles. Use a small offset spatula to remove the petits fours from the cardboard and place them into small paper cupcake liners.

WHITE CHOCOLATE–CREAM CHEESE FILLING

Makes about 2 cups (454 grams)

7.8 ounces (220 grams) white chocolate, finely chopped (about 1½ cups chopped)

8 ounces (227 grams) cream cheese

1 teaspoon (4 grams) pure vanilla extract

¼ teaspoon (1 gram) fleur de sel

Melt the chocolate over a double boiler (see page 18) until it looks to be about half-way melted. Remove it from the heat and stir it with a heat-resistant spatula until completely smooth and melted throughout. Stir in the cream cheese, then the vanilla and fleur de sel.

ORANGE FONDANT

Makes about 1¾ cups (570 grams)

2½ cups (500 grams) granulated sugar

1 cup (180 grams) freshly squeezed orange juice (from 3 or 4 medium oranges)

½ cup (85 grams) light corn syrup

½ teaspoon (2 grams) fine sea salt

1 to 3 drops orange liquid, paste, or gel food color (as desired)

Place the sugar in a medium saucepan, then slowly and carefully pour the orange juice in a spiral motion from the edges of the pan to its center, without moving the pan. Add the corn syrup and salt. Clip a calibrated candy thermometer to the pan and cook over medium heat until the sugar reaches 237°F (114°C). If the sugar is not all dissolved as it cooks, stir it gently and clean any crystals that form on the sides of the pan with a pastry brush dipped in water.

Once ready, pour the fondant into the bowl of an electric mixer, insert the thermometer into it, and let it cool at room temperature until it reaches 120°F (49°C), without stirring. Set the mixer with the paddle attachment, add the food coloring to the fondant, and beat it on medium-low speed for about 25 minutes, until it turns into a thick and opaque paste. Use immediately.

TO USE THE FONDANT: Check a bit with a spoon—the fondant should have the fluidity of a ganache and be opaque. It should coat the back of the spoon to the point that you no longer see the wood or metal. If necessary, add a few drops of water at a time to thin it out. If you add too much water, you risk overthinning the fondant, which may cause drips as you dip. When the fondant is correctly thinned out, it should cover a cake without being so thin as to be translucent or so thick as to pile up.

Milk Chocolate–Lime Caramels

CARAMELS

CHOCOLATE-CINNAMON CARAMELS

BLOOD ORANGE–CHOCOLATE CARAMELS

MILK CHOCOLATE–LIME CARAMELS

COFFEE CARAMELS

FLEUR DE SEL CARAMELS

CARAMELS ARE ONE OF MY FAVORITE INDULGENCES. AS A CHILD, I LOVED CHEWY, crisp caramel-dipped apples, and as a working pastry chef love making nut-caramel turtles dipped in chocolate. Pastry shops around the country sell great-quality flavored caramels—the flavor possibilities of caramels are seemingly endless—but if you too like to indulge, it's more budget-friendly to learn to make your own. Serve them as is on a beautiful platter or individually wrap each one for a memorable hostess gift, whether you bring it to someone's house or hand them to your guests as they leave yours.

Don't be afraid of the temperature to which you need to bring the ingredients. The mixture will turn dark when the sugar and milk solids brown, but keep stirring with a heat-resistant spatula. Never scrape the bottom of a pan when making caramel: Sugar's crystal structure varies at different temperatures, and scraping what was hotter at the bottom back into the whole batch may cause it to become grainy. If something is stuck at the bottom of the pot, pour the useable caramel out and work with that. You can cool the pan a few minutes and eat the rest out with a spoon. The easiest way to clean a pot filled with caramel or other sugar syrup is to fill it with water and boil it clean.

Chocolate-Cinnamon Caramels

These caramels make me think of the flavor of churros (fried dough rolled in cinnamon sugar) filled with chocolate. Infusing the cream with cinnamon sticks (not ground cinnamon) results in a finer texture in the finished caramels.

Makes 36 (1¼-inch/3-centimeter) caramels

1½ cups (360 grams) heavy whipping cream

8 sticks cinnamon

½ cup (165 grams) honey

½ cup (100 grams) granulated sugar

1.8 ounces (50 grams) semisweet chocolate, finely chopped (about ⅓ cup chopped)

1 teaspoon (4 grams) pure vanilla extract

¼ teaspoon (2 grams) fine sea salt

Vegetable oil cooking spray

Place the cream and cinnamon sticks in a medium saucepan over medium-high heat and bring to a boil. Remove from the heat and let the mixture steep for 30 minutes, then remove the cinnamon sticks. Gently whisk in the honey and sugar until combined, then place the pot back on the stove over medium heat. Use a heat-resistant spatula to stir the mixture in a figure-eight motion until everything is dissolved, making sure to stay about ½ inch (1.25 centimeters) away from the sides of the pot. When the mixture comes to a boil, stop stirring and clean the sides of the pot with a clean pastry brushed dipped in water.

Prepare a small bowl of ice water.

Clip a calibrated candy thermometer to the pan, and continue cooking the mixture, stirring constantly all around the pan with a heat-resistant spatula, until it reaches 244°F (118°C). Drop a small amount into ice water; it should hold a firm ball after it cools for 20 seconds. Remove from the heat and add the chocolate, vanilla, and salt, shaking the pan so that the chocolate is submerged. Let sit for 1 minute, then whisk from the center outward until the mixture is thoroughly combined and shiny.

Spray an 8-inch (20-centimeter) square pan with vegetable oil cooking spray. Pour the caramel in the pan and let it cool and set for 2 hours.

Once set, unmold the caramel onto a cutting board and cut it into 1¼-inch (3-centimeter) squares. Serve them at room temperature. The caramels can be individually wrapped in cellophane or waxed paper and stored in an airtight container at room temperature for up to 2 weeks.

Variation

BLOOD ORANGE–CHOCOLATE CARAMELS

Substitute ¾ cup (120 grams) of freshly squeezed and strained blood orange juice (from about 5 blood oranges) for ½ cup (120 grams) of the heavy whipping cream. Add the finely grated zest of 1 blood orange (4 grams). Substitute ⅓ cup (60 grams) of finely chopped white chocolate and 2 tablespoons (20 grams) of cocoa butter (see Resources, page 288) for the semisweet chocolate.

Variation

MILK CHOCOLATE–LIME CARAMELS

Reduce the amount of heavy whipping cream to 1⅛ cups (270 grams). Add the juice of 2 limes (3 generous tablespoons, about 50 grams). Substitute ⅓ cup (2 ounces, or 50 grams) of finely chopped milk chocolate for the semisweet chocolate.

Coffee Caramels

I can think of few ways to be a better hostess than to bring coffee-flavored caramels along when I serve visitors coffee. It immediately makes them feel special and can transport them onto the *terrasse* of a café in Paris with just a simple gesture.

Makes 36 (1¼-inch/3-centimeter) caramels

1½ cups (360 grams) heavy whipping cream

½ cup (165 grams) honey

½ cup (100 grams) granulated sugar

1 tablespoon (3 grams) espresso powder

2 tablespoons (20 grams) cocoa butter
(see Resources, page 288)

1 teaspoon (4 grams) pure vanilla extract

¼ teaspoon (2 grams) fine sea salt

Vegetable oil cooking spray

Place the cream, honey, and sugar in a medium saucepan over medium heat and gently whisk them to combine. Use a heat-resistant spatula to stir the mixture in a figure-eight motion until everything is dissolved, making sure to stay about ½ inch (1.25 centimeters) away from the sides of the pot. When the mixture comes to a boil, stop stirring and clean the sides of the pot with a pastry brush dipped in water.

Prepare a small bowl of ice water.

Clip a calibrated candy thermometer to the pan, and continue cooking the mixture, stirring constantly all around the pan with a heat-resistant spatula, until it reaches 244°F (118°C). Drop a small amount into ice water; it should hold a firm ball after it cools for 20 seconds. Remove from the heat and immediately stir in the espresso powder, cocoa butter, vanilla, and salt until the mixture is thoroughly combined.

Spray an 8-inch (20-centimeter) square pan with vegetable oil cooking spray. Pour the caramel in the pan and let it cool and set for 2 hours.

Once set, unmold the caramel onto a cutting board and cut it into 1¼-inch (3-centimeter) squares. Serve them at room temperature. The caramels can be individually wrapped in cellophane or waxed paper and stored in an airtight container at room temperature for up to 2 weeks.

Variation

FLEUR DE SEL CARAMELS

Omit the espresso powder and fine sea salt. After pouring the cooked caramel into the prepared pan, sprinkle a rounded ¼ teaspoon (1 gram) of fleur de sel evenly over the warm caramel.

Green Apple–Yuzu Marshmallows

MARSHMALLOWS

FRANCE IS KNOWN FOR ITS HIGH-QUALITY *GUIMAUVE*, WHICH IS, AS IT IS HERE, A beloved kids' treat. Whether they are to dress up a thick, homemade hot chocolate or to bring out on a tray with coffee, marshmallows are another treat that can take on nearly all of your favorite flavors. I particularly like playing with slightly tart or bitter ingredients, since marshmallows are so sweet. They are named for the sap of the mallow plant, an antique thickener. Modern recipes are typically gelatin based and made with or without egg whites. Egg whites make for a slightly fluffier marshmallow, but egg-free ones last longer, which is why

I decided to feature those here. Have fun with their shapes: You can use cookie cutters or make long sticks that you then arrange in a tower shape on a dessert buffet. Take a piece from the three-Michelin-star Jean-Georges's playbook and cut them from a long stick at the table for your guests at the end of a dinner party. Wrapped in a beautiful little bag, they make for an original and sophisticated hostess gift that will please children and grown-ups alike.

Grapefruit-Anise Marshmallows

Anise liqueur is as French a spirit as they come—Pastis is a common brand, even here. It turns a characteristic milky white when mixed with water and because it is refreshing, is often drunk in the warm South of France. Paired with grapefruit, it makes for a slightly bittersweet marshmallow, which I love. You can use other liqueurs, such as Campari, which will give the marshmallows a nice orangey color.

Makes 16 (2-inch/5-centimeter) marshmallows

1 cup (240 grams) freshly squeezed and strained grapefruit juice (from 1 large grapefruit), divided

1 tablespoon plus 1 teaspoon (13 grams) granulated plain gelatin

2 cups (400 grams) granulated sugar

½ cup (170 grams) light corn syrup

Finely grated zest of ½ grapefruit (4 grams)

2 teaspoons (10 grams) anise liqueur, such as Pastis

⅛ cup (19 grams) confectioners' sugar

Place ¼ cup (60 grams) of the grapefruit juice in the bowl of an electric mixer fitted with the whisk attachment and sprinkle the gelatin evenly over the juice. Whisk until the gelatin is well incorporated and let it hydrate for 5 minutes.

Place the granulated sugar, the remaining ¾ cup (180 grams) of grapefruit juice, the corn syrup, and the grapefruit zest in a small, deep saucepan. Stir carefully to combine, then clean the edges of the pan with a clean pastry brush dipped in cold water. Clip a calibrated candy thermometer to the pan and bring the mixture to a boil over medium-low heat, cooking it until it reaches 235°F (113°C). Hold at that temperature for 1 minute to ensure accuracy. Watch the mixture carefully—if it foams up, remove the pot from the heat until the bubbles subside, then continue with the recipe.

Pour the cooked syrup over the gelatin in the mixer bowl, add the anise liqueur, and whip on high speed until the mixture thickens, doubles in volume, and begins to cool, about 9 minutes in a 5-quart (4.7-liter) mixer or 6 minutes in a 6-quart (5.7-liter) mixer. When it's time to stop whipping, the marshmallow will just "ribbon" if you draw the whisk up about 2 inches (5 centimeters).

While the mixture whips, place half the confectioners' sugar in a fine-mesh sieve and heavily sprinkle an 8-inch (20-centimeter) square pan with it. Once the mixture is ready, quickly pour it into the pan. Tap the pan gently, then sift the remaining confectioners' sugar over the marshmallow. Let it set for 2 hours at room temperature.

Once set, use a bench scraper to cut around the edges of the pan and break the vacuum seal that keeps the marshmallow in the pan. Place the marshmallow slab on a cutting board and with a chef's knife, cut it into 2-inch (5-centimeter) squares. Dust off any excess confectioners' sugar with a pastry brush. The marshmallows will keep for 2 weeks in an airtight container at room temperature.

Green Apple–Yuzu Marshmallows

Tart, crisp green apple and yuzu cut through the inherent sweetness of marshmallows. You will find bottled yuzu juice in Asian supermarkets and online. You can also substitute freshly squeezed lime juice—but do not use bottled lime juice, as the flavor will not be good—or passion fruit juice. To make your own green apple purée, peel the apples, remove the seeds, and run them through a food processor. Both commercial and homemade purée slightly oxidize and turn a bit brown, but the flavor will be great. Regular applesauce has been cooked, so don't substitute that.

Makes 16 (2-inch/5-centimeter) marshmallows

2 tablespoons (24 grams) water

2 teaspoons (10 grams) yuzu juice (see headnote)

1 tablespoon plus 1 teaspoon (13 grams) granulated plain gelatin

2 cups (400 grams) granulated sugar

¾ cup (240 grams) green apple purée
(see Resources, page 288, or make your own)

½ cup (170 grams) light corn syrup

⅛ cup (19 grams) confectioners' sugar

3 or 4 drops green liquid, paste, or
gel food coloring (as desired)

Place the water and yuzu juice in the bowl of an electric mixer fitted with the whisk attachment and sprinkle the gelatin evenly over the liquids. Whisk until the gelatin is well incorporated and let it hydrate for 5 minutes.

Place the granulated sugar, apple purée, and corn syrup in a small, deep saucepan. Stir carefully to combine, then clean the edges of the pan with a clean pastry brush dipped in cold water. Clip a calibrated candy thermometer to the pan and bring the mixture to a boil over medium-low heat, cooking it until it reaches 235°F (113°C). Hold at that temperature for 1 minute to ensure accuracy. Watch the mixture carefully—if it foams up, remove the pot from the heat until the bubbles subside, then continue with the recipe.

Pour the cooked syrup over the gelatin in the mixer bowl and whip on high speed until the mixture thickens, doubles in volume, and begins to cool, about 9 minutes in a 5-quart (4.7-liter) mixer or 6 minutes in a 6-quart (5.7-liter) mixer. When it's time to stop whipping, the marshmallow will just "ribbon" if you draw the whisk up about 2 inches (5 centimeters).

While the mixture whips, place the confectioners' sugar in a fine-mesh sieve and heavily sprinkle an 8-inch (20-centimeter) square pan with it. Once the mixture is ready, quickly pour two-thirds of it into the pan. Stir the food coloring into the remaining mixture, then swirl it over the top of the plain marshmallow. Run the tip of a paring knife around the pan to create a marbleized marshmallow.

Tap the pan gently, then sift the remaining confectioners' sugar over the marshmallow. Let it set overnight preferably, but at least 8 hours at room temperature.

Once set, use a bench scraper to cut around the edges of the pan and break the vacuum seal that keeps the marshmallow in the pan. Place the marshmallow slab on a cutting board and with a chef's knife, cut it into 2-inch (5-centimeter) squares. Dust off any excess confectioners' sugar with a pastry brush. The marshmallows will keep for 2 weeks in an airtight container at room temperature.

Apricot–Blood Orange Marshmallows

Blood oranges and apricots have almost opposite seasons, but I usually freeze blood orange juice to have on hand more than a few weeks a year. Both ingredients are sweetly tart, which I find makes them work well together. You can make this recipe anytime by using regular orange juice and canned apricots (well drained and puréed), however. These marshmallows have a wonderful, soft shade of orange without adding any food coloring.

Makes 16 (2-inch/5-centimeter) marshmallows

⅔ cup (120 grams) freshly squeezed and strained blood orange juice (from 3 or 4 blood oranges)

1 tablespoon (10 grams) granulated plain gelatin

2 cups (400 grams) granulated sugar

½ cup (115 grams) apricot purée (see Resources, page 288)

½ cup (170 grams) light corn syrup

⅛ cup (19 grams) confectioners' sugar

Place the blood orange juice in the bowl of an electric mixer fitted with the whisk attachment and sprinkle the gelatin evenly over the juice. Whisk until the gelatin is well incorporated and let it hydrate for 5 minutes.

Place the granulated sugar, apricot purée, and corn syrup in a small, deep saucepan. Stir carefully to combine, then clean the edges of the pan with a clean pastry brush dipped in cold water. Clip a calibrated candy thermometer to the pan and bring the mixture to a boil over medium-low heat, cooking it until it reaches 235°F (113°C). Hold at that temperature for 1 minute to ensure accuracy. Watch the mixture carefully—if it foams up, remove the pot from the heat until the bubbles subside, then continue with the recipe.

Pour the cooked syrup over the gelatin in the mixer bowl and whip on high speed until the mixture thickens, doubles in volume, and begins to cool, about 9 minutes in a 5-quart (4.7-liter) mixer or 6 minutes in a 6-quart (5.7-liter) mixer. When it's time to stop whipping, the marshmallow will just "ribbon" if you draw the whisk up about 2 inches (5 centimeters).

While the mixture whips, place the confectioners' sugar in a fine-mesh sieve and heavily sprinkle an 8-inch (20-centimeter) square pan with it. Once the mixture is ready, quickly pour it into the pan.

Tap the pan gently, then sift the remaining confectioners' sugar over the marshmallow. Let it set overnight preferably, but at least 8 hours at room temperature.

Once set, use a bench scraper to cut around the edges of the pan and break the vacuum seal that keeps the marshmallow in the pan. Place the marshmallow slab on a cutting board and with a chef's knife, cut it into 2-inch (5-centimeter) squares. Dust off any excess confectioners' sugar with a pastry brush. The marshmallows will keep for 2 weeks in an airtight container at room temperature.

Lavender-Honey Marshmallows

Lavender honey is abundant in the South of France, where bees can feed on fields of lavender that go as far as the eye can see—that's where I'm transported when I make and eat these marshmallows. If you can't find it, use clover or wildflower honey instead. When cooking with flowers, as is the case here, check that they are of the edible kind. Use organic varieties to be sure they have not been treated with pesticides.

Makes 16 (2-inch/5-centimeter) marshmallows

½ cup (116 grams) water, divided

1 tablespoon (10 grams) granulated plain gelatin

2 cups (400 grams) granulated sugar

½ vanilla bean

½ cup (165 grams) lavender honey

Scant ¼ teaspoon (0.125 gram) dried lavender buds

⅛ cup (19 grams) confectioners' sugar

3 to 4 drops purple liquid, paste, or gel food coloring (as desired)

Place ¼ cup (58 grams) of the water in the bowl of an electric mixer fitted with the whisk attachment and sprinkle the gelatin evenly over the liquid. Whisk until the gelatin is well incorporated and let it hydrate for 5 minutes.

Place the granulated sugar in a small, deep saucepan. Split the vanilla bean lengthwise and scrape out the seeds with the back of a paring knife into the sugar. Add the scraped bean to the pot. Pour the remaining ¼ cup (58 grams) of water around the edges of the pan, and swirl it into the center by tilting the pot. Clip a calibrated candy thermometer to the pan and bring the mixture to a boil over medium-low heat. When it begins to boil, pour in the honey and continue cooking the syrup until it reaches 235°F (113°C). Hold at that temperature for 1 minute to ensure accuracy. Watch the mixture carefully—if it foams up, remove the pot from the heat until the bubbles subside, then continue with the recipe. Use tongs to quickly remove the vanilla bean.

Pour the cooked syrup over the gelatin in the mixer bowl, add the lavender buds, and whip on high speed until the mixture thickens, doubles in volume, and begins to cool, about 9 minutes in a 5-quart (4.7-liter) mixer or 6 minutes in a 6-quart (5.7-liter) mixer. When it's time to stop whipping, the marshmallow will just "ribbon" if you draw the whisk up about 2 inches (5 centimeters).

While the mixture whips, place the confectioners' sugar in a fine-mesh sieve and heavily sprinkle an 8-inch (20-centimeter) square pan with it. Once the mixture is ready, quickly pour two-thirds of it into the pan. Stir the food coloring into the remaining mixture, then swirl it over the top of the plain marshmallow. Run the tip of a paring knife around the pan to create a marbleized marshmallow.

Tap the pan gently, then sift the remaining confectioners' sugar over the marshmallow. Let it set overnight preferably, but at least 8 hours at room temperature.

Once set, use a bench scraper to cut around the edges of the pan and break the vacuum seal that keeps the marshmallow in the pan. Place the marshmallow slab on a cutting board and with a chef's knife, cut it into 2-inch (5-centimeter) squares. Dust off any excess confectioners' sugar with a pastry brush. The marshmallows will keep for 2 weeks in an airtight container at room temperature.

Variation

BUCKWHEAT HONEY MARSHMALLOWS

Omit the vanilla bean, lavender buds, and food coloring. Substitute buckwheat honey for the lavender honey. Pour all the marshmallow mixture into the pan at once.

NOTE: Any strongly flavored honey may be substituted, such as pine or rosemary.

Sesame-Apricot-Rose Nougats

NOUGATS

CARDAMOM-MOCHA-ORANGE NOUGATS

CINNAMON-ORANGE–CACAO NIB NOUGATS

FIG-CHERRY-PISTACHIO-CHOCOLATE NOUGATS

ROASTED PEANUT–MILK CHOCOLATE NOUGATS

SESAME-APRICOT-ROSE NOUGATS

I VISITED MONTÉLIMAR, THE TOWN IN PROVENCE WHERE NOUGAT SUPPOSEDLY originated, several years ago and still remember the way the smell of honey permeated every street corner. Every shop was festooned with a banner proclaiming its recipe to be *the* original. Nougat is much more popular in Europe than it is here: Italy and Spain also have their versions, sold in long bars. It is available that way in France, too, but many pastry shops and open-air markets sell it in bulk in cheese-shape wheels and slice it fresh for customers, or feature towering pyramids of bite-size pieces.

The base of nougat is a honey syrup cooked to the hard-ball point, which leaves it a little soft and chewy, in the French style (it is easier to eat that way, too), flavored with a variety of ingredients. The acidity of dried tart fruits and dark chocolate cuts through the overall sweetness, for example. Try the many flavor variations offered here and then make up your own. You can cut nougat into individual pieces with a knife or a cookie cutter, having some fun in the process. Wrap them in individual pieces of cellophane and arrange them in a pretty bag or box for a perfect hostess gift.

Wafer paper helps give structure to the nougat. Make sure to use the special wafer paper made for confectionary products, which is not the same as the paper used for spring rolls—that one won't work. You can skip the paper and roll the nougat in confectioners' sugar, but the result won't be as pretty.

The process to make nougat looks overwhelming at first, but you will realize as soon as you do it once that it's not very complicated and that the mixer (and time) does much of the work for you. It's worth a try, and anyone who will receive your homemade nougat will be greatly impressed.

Cardamom-Mocha-Orange Nougats

At first glance, these nougats have a lot going on flavorwise, but fear not, it's a complementary combination of ingredients. The orange nuance comes from both orange blossom honey and orange confit, while chocolate and espresso beans add both flavor and a caffeine kick. You can use store-bought orange confit or make your own. Crush the cardamom pods with a rolling pin or the back of a spoon. The honey goes in one pot and the cardamom syrup in the other. They need to cook simultaneously, but the honey will be ready first.

Makes 24 (1¼-inch/3-centimeter) squares

⅔ cup (150 grams) water

12 green cardamom pods, crushed

2 large egg whites

½ cup (165 grams) orange blossom honey

1 cup (200 grams) granulated sugar

2 (11 x 8½-inch/28 x 22-centimeter) sheets wafer paper (see Resources, page 288)

1 teaspoon (4 grams) pure vanilla extract

½ cup (75 grams) almonds, toasted (see page 20) and chopped

½ cup (80 grams) Orange Confit (recipe follows), chopped

¼ cup (68 grams) chocolate-covered espresso beans, coarsely chopped

Scant ½ teaspoon (0.5 gram) espresso powder

0.6 ounce (18 grams) espresso-flavored chocolate (see Resources, page 288), coarsely chopped (about ½ cup chopped)

Place the water and cardamom pods in a small, deep saucepan and bring to a boil over medium-high heat. Once the mixture boils, turn off the heat and let it infuse for 10 minutes.

In the bowl of an electric mixer fitted with the whisk attachment, begin to whisk the egg whites on medium speed until soft peaks form, about 2 minutes. Reduce the speed to low if the egg whites are at soft peaks before the syrup is ready.

While the egg whites are whipping, clip a calibrated candy thermometer to the side of a small saucepan. Place the honey in the pan and heat over medium heat.

When the honey reaches 230°F (110°C), turn your attention back to the cardamom infusion. Remove the cardamom pods with a spoon and add the sugar. Heat over medium heat and stir carefully, avoiding the sides of the pan. Clean the sides of the pot with a clean pastry brush dipped in water. Since the honey will be done before the syrup, clip the same candy thermometer to the side of the syrup pot afterward.

When the honey reaches 250°F (121°C), quickly and steadily pour it down the side of the mixer bowl, with the mixer running at low speed. Rest the lip of the saucepan on the side of the bowl so the honey does not hit the whisk attachment and splatter (it should run gradually down the side of the bowl).

Once the cardamom syrup reaches 282°F (139°C), follow the same procedure to pour it into the egg whites.

Increase the mixer speed to medium and whip until the meringue cools, thickens, and becomes stiff and shiny, about 25 minutes.

Line a dry surface with waxed or parchment paper. Place one sheet of the wafer paper, shiny-side up, on top of the waxed or parchment paper.

Stop the mixer and remove the bowl from the stand (unhook the whisk attachment, which you don't need anymore). Working quickly, use a spatula to stir in the vanilla, almonds, orange confit, coffee beans, espresso powder, and chocolate.

With a bowl scraper, scoop out the nougat onto the wafer paper. Place the second sheet, shiny-side down, on top of the nougat, then roll out the nougat flat until it is about ¾ inch (2 centimeters) thick. Let set for 2 hours at room temperature, then cut the nougat into pieces (with a knife if you want squares, rectangles, or diamonds [see Calissons, page 90, for the cutting technique], or with a cookie cutter for any other shapes). Store in an airtight container at room temperature for up to 2 weeks.

WHAT SHOULD NOUGAT FEEL LIKE?

When the bottom of the mixer bowl feels lukewarm, test the texture of the nougat: Stop the mixer and drop a spoonful of the nougat into a bowl of ice water. After cooling for 20 seconds, the nougat should hold its shape and you should be able to cut cleanly through it without it softening. If it is not yet ready, return the bowl to the mixer and continue whipping on medium-high speed until you successfully repeat the test.

ORANGE CONFIT

Makes about 1¾ cups (300 grams) drained

Peels from 3 oranges (about 2½ cups, or 266 grams)

Pinch of salt

1 cup (200 grams) granulated sugar

½ cup (115 grams) water

¼ cup (85 grams) light corn syrup

Cut the orange peels into ¼-inch (6-millimeter)-wide strips, then cut those into ¼-inch (6-millimeter) pieces. Place the peels in a small stainless-steel saucepan. Add the salt and enough cold water to cover. Bring to a boil over medium-high heat and blanch for 5 minutes once the water is boiling. Pour the mixture into a fine-mesh strainer or a chinois and rinse in cold water. Repeat the blanching process 4 more times, without adding extra salt. The last time, leave the peels in the strainer and reserve.

Pour the sugar and water into the saucepan and bring to a boil over medium-high heat with the corn syrup and blanched orange peels. Once the mixture is boiling, lower the heat to low and let simmer for 20 minutes. Remove the pan from the heat and cover it. Let the mixture cool overnight in the syrup. Store the cooled confit in the refrigerator for up to 3 months. Drain the peel before adding it to recipes.

Variation

CINNAMON-ORANGE–CACAO NIB NOUGATS

Substitute 6 sticks of cinnamon for the cardamom pods. Substitute ¼ cup (35 grams) of caramelized cacao nibs (see Resources, page 288) for the chocolate-covered espresso beans. Omit the espresso-flavored chocolate.

Fig-Cherry-Pistachio-Chocolate Nougats

Loaded with dried fruits, nuts, and dark chocolate, this nougat could almost pass for a trail mix or energy bar—just a much more enjoyable one.

Makes 24 (1¼-inch/3-centimeter) squares

1 cup (200 grams) granulated sugar

1 vanilla bean

⅓ cup (75 grams) water

2 large egg whites

½ cup (165 grams) orange blossom honey

2 (11 x 8½-inch/28 x 22-centimeter) sheets wafer paper (see Resources, page 288)

1 tablespoon (15 grams) Grand Marnier

½ teaspoon (2 grams) finely grated orange zest (from ¼ orange)

⅛ teaspoon (0.5 gram) fleur de sel

½ cup (75 grams) pistachios, toasted (see page 20)

½ cup (63 grams) dried cherries, cut in ¼-inch (6-millimeter) pieces

⅓ cup (50 grams) dried figs, cut in ¼-inch (6-millimeter) pieces

2.7 ounces (75 grams) bittersweet chocolate, coarsely chopped (about ½ cup chopped)

Pour the sugar into a small, deep saucepan. Split the vanilla bean lengthwise and scrape out the seeds with the back of a paring knife into the sugar. Rub the bean into the sugar to scrape out more vanilla seeds. Pour the water around the edges of the pan, and swirl it into the center by tilting the pot to dissolve the sugar.

In the bowl of an electric mixer fitted with the whisk attachment, begin to whisk the egg whites on medium speed until soft peaks form, about 2 minutes. Reduce the speed to low if the egg whites are at soft peaks before the syrup is ready.

While the egg whites are whipping, clip a calibrated candy thermometer to the side of a small saucepan. Place the honey in the pan and heat over medium heat.

When the honey reaches 230°F (110°C), turn your attention back to the vanilla mixture. Heat over medium heat and stir carefully, avoiding the sides of the pan. Clean the sides with a clean pastry brush dipped in some water. Since the honey will be done before the vanilla syrup, clip the same candy thermometer to the side of the syrup pot afterward.

When the honey reaches 250°F (121°C), quickly and steadily pour it down the side of the mixer bowl, with the mixer running at low speed. Rest the lip of the saucepan on the side of the bowl so the honey does not hit the whisk attachment and splatter (it should run gradually down the side of the bowl).

Once the vanilla syrup reaches 282°F (139°C), quickly remove the vanilla bean with kitchen tongs and follow the same procedure to pour it into the egg whites.

Increase the mixer speed to medium and whip until the meringue cools, thickens, and becomes stiff and shiny, about 25 minutes.

Line a dry surface with waxed or parchment paper. Place one sheet of the wafer paper, shiny-side up, on top of the waxed or parchment paper.

Stop the mixer and remove the bowl from the stand (unhook the whisk attachment, which you don't need anymore). Working quickly, use a spatula to stir in the Grand Marnier, orange zest, fleur de sel, pistachios, cherries, and figs. Once everything is thoroughly mixed, stir in the chocolate.

With a bowl scraper, scoop out the nougat onto the wafer paper. Place the second sheet, shiny-side down, on top of the nougat, then roll out the nougat flat until it is about ¾ inch (2 centimeters) thick. Let set for 2 hours at room temperature, then cut the nougat into pieces (with a knife if you want squares, rectangles, or diamonds [see Calissons, page 90, for the cutting technique], or with a cookie cutter for any other shapes). Store in an airtight container at room temperature for up to 2 weeks.

Variation

ROASTED PEANUT–MILK CHOCOLATE NOUGATS

Omit the vanilla bean. Substitute pure vanilla extract for the Grand Marnier. Add ⅛ teaspoon (0.5 gram) of fleur de sel with the vanilla extract. Replace the pistachios, cherries, and figs with 1 cup (165 grams) of honey-roasted peanuts. Substitute milk chocolate for the bittersweet, and add 1 cup (25 grams) of cornflakes and ½ cup (78 grams) of raisins with the chocolate and peanuts.

Sesame-Apricot-Rose Nougats

Sesame, rose, and apricots are typical Middle Eastern flavors. This is a take on Turkish delights—*loukoums* in France, where they are very popular. Cutting them exposes the sesame seeds and rose petals, which makes for an exceptionally pretty nougat.

Makes 24 (1¼-inch/3 centimeter) squares

1 cup (200 grams) granulated sugar

⅓ cup (75 grams) water

2 large egg whites

½ cup (165 grams) orange blossom honey

2 (11 x 8½-inch/28 x 22-centimeter) sheets wafer paper (see Resources, page 288)

1 teaspoon (5 grams) rose water

½ teaspoon (2 grams) pure vanilla extract

¼ teaspoon (2 grams) finely grated orange zest (from ¼ orange)

¼ teaspoon (1 gram) finely grated lemon zest (from ¼ lemon)

⅛ teaspoon (0.5 gram) fleur de sel

1¼ cups (275 grams) dried apricots, cut in ¼-inch (6-millimeter) pieces

½ cup (60 grams) sesame seeds, toasted (see page 20)

½ cup (60 grams) black sesame seeds, toasted (see page 20)

1 teaspoon (0.5 gram) organic red or pink rose petals

Pour the sugar into a small, deep saucepan, then pour the water around the edges of the pan and swirl it into the center by tilting the pot to dissolve the sugar.

In the bowl of an electric mixer fitted with the whisk attachment, begin to whisk the egg whites on medium speed until soft peaks form, about 2 minutes. Reduce the speed to low if the egg whites are at soft peaks before the syrup is ready.

While the egg whites are whipping, clip a calibrated candy thermometer to the side of a small saucepan. Place the honey in the pan and heat over medium heat.

When the honey reaches 230°F (110°C), turn your attention back to the sugar mixture. Heat over medium heat and stir carefully, avoiding the sides of the pan. Clean the sides of the pot with a clean pastry brush dipped in some water. Since the honey will be done before the syrup, clip the same candy thermometer to the side of the syrup pot afterward.

When the honey reaches 250°F (121°C), quickly and steadily pour it down the side of the mixer bowl, with the mixer running at low speed. Rest the lip of the saucepan on the side of the bowl so the honey does not hit the whisk attachment and splatter (it should run gradually down the side of the bowl).

Once the syrup reaches 282°F (139°C), follow the same procedure to pour it into the egg whites.

Increase the mixer speed to medium and whip until the meringue cools, thickens, and becomes stiff and shiny, about 25 minutes.

Line a dry surface with waxed or parchment paper. Place one sheet of the wafer paper, shiny-side up, on top of the waxed or parchment paper.

Stop the mixer and remove the bowl from the stand (unhook the whisk attachment, which you don't need anymore). Working quickly, use a spatula to stir in the rose water, vanilla, orange and lemon zests, fleur de sel, apricots, and both types of sesame seeds. Once everything is thoroughly mixed, carefully stir in the rose petals.

With a bowl scraper, scoop out the nougat onto the wafer paper. Place the second sheet, shiny-side down, on top of the nougat, then roll out the nougat flat until it is about ¾ inch (2 centimeters) thick. Let set for 2 hours at room temperature, then cut the nougat into pieces (with a knife if you want squares, rectangles, or diamonds [see Calissons, page 90, for the cutting technique], or with a cookie cutter for any other shapes). Store in an airtight container at room temperature for up to 2 weeks.

Blackberry-Apricot Pâtes de Fruits

Pâtes de Fruits

BLACKBERRY-APRICOT PÂTES DE FRUITS

MANGO-BANANA PÂTES DE FRUITS

PEAR-CRANBERRY PÂTES DE FRUITS

CASSIS-APPLE PÂTES DE FRUITS

RASPBERRY-CHERRY PÂTES DE FRUITS

ENDING A DINNER BY PLACING THESE DELICATE, FRUIT-BASED CONFECTIONS ON the table will make any home feel like a four-star restaurant. I first made and fell in love with pâtes de fruits while working at the Rainbow Room, where as a lowly pastry cook I was able to express my creativity by using all sorts of fruits. Think of it as the ancestor of the gumdrop or as a more grown-up gummy bear. Your tooth first encounters the slightest resistance at the surface, which then becomes a soft and sweet center that almost melts in your mouth.

Making pâte de fruit resembles the jam-making process, with the mixture cooking to a slightly tighter point—the finished pâtes de fruits should be moist and still have a bit of looseness to them, while holding together unmistakably more than jam. The more natural pectin a fruit contains, the less commercial pectin you need to add to transform the fruit purée into a pâte de fruit (which translates literally as "fruit paste"). Its gelling nature allows you to mold it in any shape you'd like by letting the mixture set in the silicone mold with bite-size cavities of your choosing; the total yield will vary depending on the size of the mold. Silicone molds are widely available in a variety of shapes; try semisphere, pyramid, or log shapes. Or cut them in classic square or rectangle shapes.

A NOTE ABOUT YELLOW PECTIN

Yellow pectin is a slow-setting, nonreversible gelling agent processed from citrus fruits or apples. It is used for jams, jellies, and pâtes de fruit, and works particularly well with fruits that have a higher water content, such as strawberries. You can order it online (see Resources, page 288). If you substitute regular pectin, the pâtes de fruit might set too loosely.

Blackberry-Apricot Pâtes de Fruits

Pâtes de fruits are inherently sweet, due to their high sugar content, so I like to use fruits that are a bit on the tart side. For each recipe that follows, you can purchase fruit purées (see Resources, page 288), or make your own with the directions provided. Here, purée the drained canned apricots and frozen berries that you let thaw, then strain through a fine-mesh sieve after puréeing. To give the pâtes de fruit extra texture, you can toss them in a bit of granulated sugar once they are cooled and set. It will give them a slight crunch, which contrasts nicely with the soft interior.

Makes about 18 (1-inch/2.5-centimeter) squares
or 12 (1¼-inch/3-centimeter) silicone-molded shapes

1½ cups (300 grams) granulated sugar, plus more as needed

½ teaspoon (2 grams) yellow pectin (see facing page)

1½ cups (400 grams) apricot purée

½ cup (150 grams) blackberry purée

1 teaspoon (4 grams) freshly squeezed and strained lemon juice (from ½ lemon)

Place the sugar and pectin in a small stainless-steel saucepan and stir until completely combined. Add the apricot and blackberry purées and bring to a boil over medium heat, stirring constantly over the whole surface of the pot with a heat-resistant spatula. Clip a calibrated candy thermometer to the pan and continue cooking the mixture, stirring constantly, until it reaches 222°F (106°C) or clings to the spatula, about 20 minutes. The mixture will be dark and thick, with large, slow-bursting bubbles. It will thicken considerably as it cools, so be careful to not overcook or caramelize it.

Remove from the heat, stir in the lemon juice, and quickly pour the mixture into a mini loaf pan or into bite-size silicone molds. Let it cool completely at room temperature until it is thick and set, about 2 hours.

Once set, unmold if using a silicone mold, or use a bench scraper to cut around the edges of the pan and break the vacuum seal that keeps the pâte de fruit slab in the pan. Place the slab on a cutting board and with a chef's knife, cut it into 6 even strips widthwise and 3 even strips lengthwise, to make 1-inch (2.5-centimeter) squares. If desired, toss the pâtes de fruit in more granulated sugar. The pâtes de fruits will keep for 2 weeks in an airtight container at room temperature.

Variation

MANGO-BANANA PÂTES DE FRUITS

Replace the apricot purée with mango and the blackberry purée with banana. To make your own, purée ripe fresh mangoes and bananas in a food processor. I like the texture of the fruits, so you don't need to strain them.

AVIGNON (Vaucluse)
Le Palais des Papes (XIVe s.)
et la Cathédrale (XIIe s.)
vus du Sud-Ouest

Variation

PEAR-CRANBERRY PÂTES DE FRUITS

Replace the apricot purée with pear and the blackberry purée with cranberry. To make your own, purée ripe fresh or drained canned pears and fresh or frozen and thawed cranberries in a food processor. Do not strain. Increase the pectin to ¾ teaspoon (3 grams).

Variation

CASSIS-APPLE PÂTES DE FRUITS

Replace the apricot purée with apple and the blackberry purée with cassis (see Resources, page 288). Use apple purée or make your own (see page 255). There is no substitute for cassis purée (unless you grow your own black currants or find them at the farmers' market, but that limits you to making this recipe a few weeks in the summer), so use store-bought or if needed, keep the blackberry from the original recipe. Decrease the pectin to ⅓ teaspoon (1.5 grams).

Variation

RASPBERRY-CHERRY PÂTES DE FRUITS

Replace the apricot purée with cherry and the blackberry purée with raspberry. To make your own, purée fresh or drained canned cherries and fresh or thawed frozen raspberries in a food processor. Strain through a fine-mesh sieve after puréeing. Decrease the pectin to ⅓ teaspoon (1.5 grams).

RESOURCES

THE COMPANIES LISTED HERE ARE PRIMARILY WHOLESALERS WHO SELL TO THE PUB-lic and retail outlets. The wholesalers may be new companies to you, but they are where chefs shop. Some will require a minimum order, but if you need more than one item it may be economical. You might also find it worth it to buy certain items in bulk.

AMERICAN ALMOND PRODUCTS COMPANY

www.americanalmond.com

(800) 825-6663

This wholesale company sells nuts and nut flours in 5- and 25-pound (2.3- and 11.3-kilogram) boxes.

AMAZON

www.amazon.com

Amazon sells nearly anything you might need to make the recipes in this book, from baking equipment, such as silicone molds in a variety of shapes and sizes, football-shaped cutters for calissons, baking sheets, and digital scales, to specialty ingredients, such as beeswax, gelatin, yeast, and Opalys, a low-sugar-added white chocolate.

CHEF RUBBER

www.shopchefrubber.com

(702) 614-9310

A good resource for unusual food colorings, including powders and glitter, as well as such equipment as digital scales.

JB PRINCE

www.jbprince.com

36 E. 31st Street, New York, NY

(800) 473-0577

This equipment retailer is a great source for baking sheets, piping bags and tips, and silicone, copper, and stainless-steel molds.

KALUSTYAN'S

www.kalustyans.com

123 Lexington Avenue, New York, NY

(800) 352-3451

This New York City store sells a number of spices online, as well as fruit purées in its freezers for local purchases.

KEREKES

www.bakedeco.com

6103 15th Avenue, Brooklyn, NY

(800) 525-5556

You will find there a large assortment of food colorings, including powders, and other equipment, such as parchment paper and piping bags.

KING ARTHUR FLOUR

www.kingarthurflour.com
135 US Rt. 5 South, Norwich, VT
(800) 827-6836
This miller of fine flours is a great source for almond and hazelnut flours, pearl sugar, almond paste, and other baking ingredients.

L'EPICERIE

www.lepicerie.com
(866) 350-7575
L'Epicerie sells smaller quantities of ingredients once sold only wholesale. It is a great source for powdered fruits, nut flours, praline paste, fruit purées, flavor compounds, essential and citrus oils, and other specialty baking ingredients.

NY CAKE & BAKING DISTRIBUTORS

www.nycake.com
56 W. 22nd Street, New York, NY
(212) 675-2253
This New York institution ships all over the world. It sells food colorings, chocolates, pearl sugar, specialty baking ingredients, and such equipment as baking sheets, silicone baking mats, parchment paper, and piping bags and tips.

SUGARPASTE/CRYSTAL COLORS

www.sugarpaste.com
(574) 233-6524
This company offers a beautiful assortment of unusual food colorings.

TRADER JOE'S

www.traderjoes.com

You will find almond and hazelnut flours, chocolates, freeze-dried berries, and other common baking and cooking ingredients at your local branch of this national retailer.

WHOLE FOODS

www.wholefoodsmarket.com

You will find almond and hazelnut flours and other common baking and cooking ingredients at your local branch of this national retailer.

ACKNOWLEDGMENTS

FROM KATHRYN AND ANNE

WE WOULD LIKE TO THANK OUR EDITOR, KRISTEN GREEN WIEWORA AT RUNning Press, who asked us to work on this second dessert book and has been as much a champion of it as she was for our first book. She is a thoughtful and generous editor who always stirs us in the right direction. It's been a great pleasure to work with her and her team again.

We would also like to thank our agent, Angela Miller, for sustaining us along the way with wise advice and ideas, and some of her delicious Consider Bardwell Farm cheeses.

A book like *Les Petits Sweets* needs an art director who understands the balance of technicality and ease of the recipes and gives them the right amount of Frenchness. Frances Soo Ping Chow at Running Press is just that person.

Photographer Evan Sung, prop stylist Maeve Sheridan, and her assistant Ashley Schleeper made for the most relaxed, efficient, and fun photoshoot authors can dream of, combining beautiful vision with patience and attention to detail. We were extraordinarily lucky to work with them and are grateful for the stunning photos that accompany the recipes.

Please visit us online at kathryn-gordon.com and annemcbride.net.

From Kathryn:

First and foremost, many thanks for the support in time, space, materials, and encouragement given to me at the Institute of Culinary Education by President Rick Smilow, Vice President of Education Richard Simpson, Dean Andrea Tutunjian, Program Director Jeff Yoskowitz, and Creative Director Michael Laiskonis. I have immense appreciation through the entire R&D phase for Sofia Yokosawa's work; she single-handedly tested the entire first fifth of the recipes. This book would not have been possible without the encouragement and palate shared by my wife, Jessie Riley; enthusiasm of friend Diane Garisto; and French inspiration given to me for the past fifteen years by Bernard Levenez. Many thanks to the crew of recipe testers who graduated from ICE and helped take the recipes through their paces at the school and in some cases even in their home ovens, including Poornima Solairajan, Michelle Effron, Theresa Battista, Kimberly A.

Coward, Nevia D. Giles, Kenyetta Acosta, Genevieve Qua, Dean Morrison, Antonette Vivas, Samantha Litchfield, Camilla Tinoco, Christina Sookhoo, Nick Rubino, Michele Schmittgall, Panfan Schnittker, Candice Radnoti (and her father, Alex Radnoti), Paulette Karam, Girika Mahajan, Maria Tillous, Kashmala Khan, Jamie French, AnnMarie Mattila, Zachary Redin, Marla Lemonik, Laura Avanessian, Gerri Lynn, Caroline Wilson, Rita Chou, Michael La Corte, Matthew Gan, Laura Velez-Paz, Claire Obias, Oprah Davidson, Ellen Relos, Loren Marino, Stacey Lu, Giuseppina Pullara, Rachel Patall-David, Michela Haller, Ritika Gupta, Gabriella Ramirez, Julian Chenov, Emilio Cura, Kelvin Ng, Nicolle Mroczek, Lauren Wong, Felicia Shields, Patty Carroll, Luz Astudillo, Papron Prabpol, Gisele Azevedo Lembi Silva, and Wayne Huang. And many thanks to my students at ICE who helped prep for the photo shoot: Dylan Rodriguez, Kathryn Green, Wendell Ashton, Shayla Watson, Stamatis Kakleas, Amanda Guerrios, Pandora Hsieh, Meng Huang, Carol Hill, Yosefa Yosi Adianto, Fred Patak, Van Trainor, and Darline Castor. Friends Daniella Tagino, Tina Korting and Mirielle Korting, and Hannah Marsland helped as recipe testers; Karen Heyson, Rita Yoskowitz, Arlene Ayoub, Kate Riley, Melody Edwards, and Dana Landis helped fill in with experimental project bits and pieces along this process. I would also like to thank Chef Rubber, American Almond, Valrhona Chocolate, NY Cake, and Ateco for their support in terms of ingredients and equipment that helped us test all the recipes successfully.

From Anne:

I am grateful to have been able to collaborate with Kathryn again and work on one of my most favorite topics. She is among the most hardworking people I know and is relentless in seeking perfection in her recipes. My family in Switzerland and France might well visit more pastry shops and eat more sweets during my visits home than they do the rest of the year but tolerate that with great patience and love, and throughout the year make my research their own; I am thankful for them beyond limits. My teenage brother, Stanislas, has fallen in love with pastry, too, and has become very adept at his own creations; he is a source of pride. François Payard is always a source of inspiration and excellence and I am grateful for the knowledge he's shared over the years. Sophie Egan, while working on her own manuscript, never failed to ask about mine and provide support and encouragement along the way. Looking to better understand the science of brown butter and financiers allowed me to nerd out with Cesar Vega, always a pleasure. Jody Eddy, whose productivity is unmatched, was for this book, as she is for all projects, the most steadfast and encouraging friend one can hope to have. I appreciate her support and friendship more than words can say. And finally, the most needed gratitude of all goes to my husband, Ron McBride, who selflessly encourages any and all of my ventures. His love is the engine of everything I do.

INDEX

Note: Page references in *italics* indicate photographs.

V

W

Y